NASCAR'S NEXT GENERATION

LARRY COTHREN
AND THE EDITORS OF *STOCK CAR RACING*

CRESTLINE

CRESTLINE

An imprint of MBI Publishing Company

Crestline books are also available at discounts in bulk quantity for industrial or sales-promotional use. For details, please contact: Special Sales Manager at MBI Publishing Company, Galtier Plaza, Suite 200, 380 Jackson Street, St. Paul, MN 55101-3885 USA.

For a free catalog, call 1-800-826-6600, or visit our website at www.motorbooks.com.

On the front cover: (clockwise from upper left) Greg Biffle, Kurt Busch, Dale Earnhardt Jr., Kevin Harvick, Jimmie Johnson, Matt Kenseth, Jamie McMurray, Ryan Newman, Elliott Sadler, and Scott Wimmer. *All photos by Nigel Kinrade.*

On the frontispiece: Since strapping into a Winston Cup car, Matt Kenseth has become one of the sport's top young drivers. *Paul Melhado*

On the title page: Drivers make their way around the track at the Daytona 500. Michael Waltrip, who recently turned 40, won the race in February 2003, but several members of NASCAR's next generation of stars followed closely behind. Kurt Busch finished second, Jimmie Johnson was third, and Kevin Harvick was fourth. *Nigel Kinrade*

On the back cover: (bottom) Jimmie Johnson or some other young driver often can be found leading the pack in a Winston Cup race. *Sam Sharpe* (top right) Johnson, who quickly became a driver that fans watch closely, discusses racing strategy with Dale Earnhardt Jr., who understands what it's like to receive the NASCAR star treatment. *Nigel Kinrade* (center) Jamie McMurray used to watch races from the stands. Now he's in the spotlight when he finishes strong. *Nigel Kinrade* (top left) Matt Kenseth, who captured the rookie of the year title in 2000, surveys the track at Kansas Speedway. *Nigel Kinrade*

Edited by Lee Klancher and Leah Noel
Designed by Katie Sonmor

ISBN 0-7603-1518-3

Printed in China

CONTENTS

INTRODUCTION

Blame it on Jeff Gordon.

If you've wondered why the starting lineups for NASCAR races have grown younger over the past decade, consider this: You can trace the sport's youth movement to a single occurrence in 1992.

Here's how it transpired. Team owner Rick Hendrick was atop a transporter watching a Busch Series practice at Atlanta Motor Speedway in '92 when he noticed a car being driven hard—right at the edge of disaster—on the 1.5-mile speedway. Two things crossed Hendrick's mind: *Who is that guy?* And, *Watch him, he's going to crash.*

Well, the driver busting those laps at Atlanta was Gordon. And, no, he didn't crash, but he did something bigger. He made an impression on Hendrick.

Through a fortuitous series of events—triggered primarily by the fact that Gordon wasn't under contract to any of Hendrick's rivals—Hendrick was able to bring Gordon and crew chief Ray Evernham onboard at Hendrick Motorsports.

Gordon catching Hendrick's eye was a watershed event for NASCAR. The teaming of Gordon, Evernham, and Hendrick set in motion events that have changed the face of the sport. Much of what we see in stock car racing today—the mainstream appeal, the choice of young drivers to fill open seats, the increased corporate involvement, and improved TV ratings—stems from that day in Atlanta.

Gordon was only 21 when he aligned with Hendrick. By the time he was 27, at the end of the 1998 season, Gordon had won three Winston Cup championships and 42 races. By age 30, even after the departure of Evernham, he had his fourth title, led by new crew chief Robbie Loomis. Amazingly, from 1996 through 1998, Gordon won 33 races, and his overall victory ledger reached 62 by the midpoint of 2003. He's now seventh on the all-time win list and the sport's winningest active driver.

Before Gordon arrived on the scene, numbers even remotely close to those were unheard of from young drivers. At an age when NASCAR competitors usually enter the most productive phase of their careers—their early 30s—Gordon was already one of the sport's greatest drivers. Only Richard Petty and Dale Earnhardt have more championships than Gordon, with seven each.

You won't find a celebration of Gordon's accomplishments in the pages of this book, but make no mistake that what you will find can be attributed directly to Gordon, who opened doors that young drivers previously did not enter in NASCAR's top division.

Dale Earnhardt Jr., Matt Kenseth, Jimmie Johnson, Ryan Newman, Kevin Harvick, and Kurt Busch are winning races and providing leadership in NASCAR. Jamie McMurray, Greg Biffle, and Elliott Sadler have demonstrated they've got what it takes to do the same. And Scott Wimmer, a rising Busch Series star, will soon join them.

Those drivers demonstrate the broad appeal of NASCAR, as they hail from all areas of the country—from Washington to North Carolina, from California to Wisconsin.

Kenseth and Biffle, each in their early 30s, are the oldest of the drivers we're calling NASCAR's next generation, and Kurt Busch, at 25, is the youngest. What they all have in common is a basic, deep-seated desire to be the best at what they do. Nevertheless, none of the drivers would be where they are without uncommon talent and fortitude. Soon, one of them will win a championship; eventually, several may be included alongside Gordon among the greatest drivers in the sport's history.

Seven of the next generation of drivers—Earnhardt Jr., Kenseth, Johnson, Newman, Harvick, Biffle, and Busch—won races as rookies in NASCAR's top division, and McMurray won in his second Winston Cup race while running a limited schedule before he even officially began his rookie season. And before they reached NASCAR's top division, Earnhardt Jr. and Kenseth helped lift the Busch Series to unprecedented popularity in the late 1990s.

The stories enclosed here, all from the pages of *Stock Car Racing* and *Circle Track* magazines, capture these young drivers in various stages of their careers. You'll find interesting stories and breathtaking photography from some of the leaders in motorsports journalism. The statistics on each driver have been compiled from official NASCAR information and the Fox Sports website.

This is an exciting time to be a follower of NASCAR racing. At no time in the sport's history have so many young competitors demonstrated as much talent and potential. They're responsible for a major portion of the sport's massive appeal and promising future.

You're sure to see one of these young drivers in a victory lane near you, and when you do, remember to give credit to Jeff Gordon.

— *Larry Cothren*

In 2002, his sophomore season, Kurt Busch came to the forefront of Winston Cup racing. He won four races, including three of the season's last five. *Nigel Kinrade*

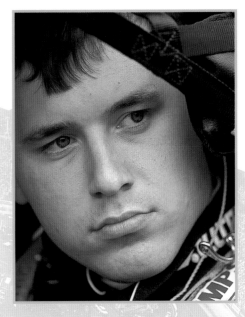

Ryan Newman was inspired to become a racing star by watching Richard Petty and Dale Earnhardt battle for wins when he was growing up.

Nigel Kinrade

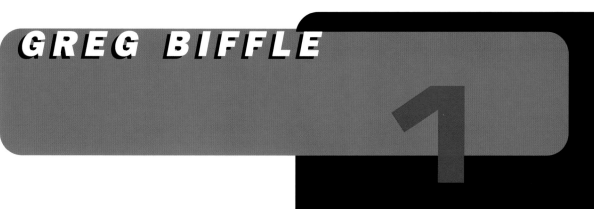

GREG BIFFLE

1

Born: December 23, 1969
Hometown: Vancouver, Washington
Height: 5-9
Weight: 170 lbs.

Sponsor	Grainger
Make	Ford
Crew Chief	Randy Goss
Owner	Geoff Smith/Jack Roush

NASCAR Winston Cup Career Statistics

Year	Races	Wins	Top 5s	Top 10s	Poles	Total Points	Final Standing	Winnings
2002	7	0	0	0	0	570	48	$373,764

Greg Biffle quickly became a driver to be reckoned with in Busch. *Sam Sharpe*

ANYTHING BUT AVERAGE

BY MARK ZESKE
From *Stock Car Racing*, March 2000

Setting Records in the NASCAR Craftsman Truck Series

Greg Biffle doesn't sound like your average NASCAR driver. Biffle speaks with a distinct accent, far different tones from the familiar southeastern twangs usually heard in garage areas. And while Biffle is many things, average will never be one of them. He defies classification.

This driver often gets lumped into a growing NASCAR demographic called West Coast racers, but he's not from the wild, wild West. Biffle's just as comfortable in Vancouver, Washington, as he is in Portland, Oregon, the border towns in which he has spent most of his life. He knows more about rain than he does the barbecue debate of beef versus pork.

But don't argue beers with him. Biffle, a teenage entrepreneur and a prodigy as a car builder, is the proud owner of Biffle's Pub & Grill in Vancouver. You can read all about the restaurant on Biffle's own website, www.gregbiffle.com.

You can also read about how Biffle was the best driver on the NASCAR Craftsman Truck Series for most of the 1999 season, winning a season-record nine races. But Biffle didn't capture the title. That championship belongs to Jack Sprague, whom Biffle respects but probably won't be inviting to party at the pub any time soon.

Biffle does have a dream that he shares with most anybody who has ever paid NASCAR membership dues. "I want to race in Winston Cup," Biffle says. "I want to be at the top. While I've had that dream for a long time, it wasn't until just recently that I ever imagined it coming true."

Biffle didn't grow up at the track dreaming of being the next Dale Earnhardt or Jeff Gordon. Biffle spent all of his youth at his parents' steel construction company, tinkering around as a fabricator, starting at the early age of eight. Not only did he become good at building things, but Biffle learned how to operate a company and work hard to achieve his goals.

In high school, Biffle kept busy with sports. He was a high jumper and a two-time wrestling state champion in the 122-pound weight class. Biffle also worked part-time at an engine shop, where his first car dreams were of glamorous street machines. One night, Biffle and his father went to a local track and got hooked. The two built a street stock together and went racing.

Consequently, when Biffle got out of high school, he started his own racing shop at 19. "It didn't really take a rocket scientist or anything to figure out it would be a good business to be into," Biffle says. "We could never get any parts when we needed them and were always forced to wait weeks to get parts from places hundreds of miles away. We just started ordering extra parts every time we ordered and built up an inventory."

Biffle helped his business by building good-looking race cars, then putting them in victory lane on a regular basis. He started racing seriously in the late-model division at Portland Speedway. In 1995, Biffle finished in a first-place tie with Larry Phillips in the NASCAR Winston Racing Series national championship for short-track drivers. Phillips won the title based on tie breakers.

"I was working or racing all seven days of the week, pretty much all day every day," Biffle says. "We'd spend 18- or 19-hour days on the weekend just traveling to a track, racing, and working on our car. Then we'd get to the shop on Mondays and we'd have everybody else's cars to work on.

"But I learned so much from having the race shop. It made me the driver I am today. And I probably would have quit racing several times, primarily because I was out of money and parts, but I went and borrowed from the inventory in the shop."

So in 1997, Biffle switched the focus of his business enterprises by buying a tavern. Because he wanted to go racing full time, Biffle needed a source of income where he didn't have to be as involved as his race shop. Eventually, he sold the race shop and became the sole owner of Biffle's Pub & Grill.

He spent 1997 racing on the NASCAR Rebco Northwest Tour Series and the NASCAR Slim Jim All-Pro circuit. But it was the Winter Heat Series in Tucson, Arizona, where he got his big break. Benny Parsons, the former Winston Cup driver who worked the Tucson races as a broadcaster, was impressed with Biffle.

Parsons lobbied Jack Roush on behalf of Biffle. Roush, who owns several Winston Cup and Craftsman truck teams, finally hired Biffle before the 1998 season to drive the No. 50 Ford, sponsored by Grainger. Biffle still can't believe his luck in landing with Roush.

"There's some good drivers out West that will never get the opportunity that I've had," Biffle says. "There's nobody out there scouting them, nobody looking for them. They'll have to make their own break, create some sort of opportunity for themselves. It will be tough."

But Biffle immediately started proving that perhaps NASCAR teams should be scouting the Great Northwest region. Biffle won Craftsman Rookie of the Year honors, grabbed a rookie-record four poles, and finished eighth in the standings. He finished second twice.

Everybody on the No. 50 Grainger team felt the future was promising. "I think I made every mistake in the book [as a rookie]," Biffle recalls. "But I learned a tremendous amount in every area, from the truck arms and the heavier trucks, to the radial tires to race strategy, you know, like saving the tire and when to pit and how to pit. I learned just a tremendous amount, and it's amazing how much one person can learn during a year. It was incredible."

No, incredible was Biffle's 1999 performance. Despite struggling in the first five races, he won at Memphis, and it was just like tapping a keg at the Biffle tavern. The victories poured freely.

Not only did Biffle top Mike Skinner's record of eight wins in a season, but he also joined Dave Rezendes as one of the only drivers in Craftsman history to win on all types of tracks (short track, road course, and superspeedway) in a single season. And when Biffle won at Indianapolis Raceway Park in August at the age of 29 years and 7 months, he became the youngest driver ever to lead the Craftsman standings.

Biffle believes the key was learning to communicate with his crew chief, Randy Goss. Mike Bliss, who also raced a truck owned by Jack Roush in 1999, claims many drivers spend their careers looking for that magic chemistry that Biffle and his team found during the summer.

"He found the feel," Bliss says. "Every driver looks for a feel that they want, and he found it. Not only that, but he could communicate it to the team. Greg and the team really developed together, and they've got something going that is really special. The team could find his feel at just about every kind of track that we raced at, which doesn't happen that often in racing."

Biffle owned the Craftsman Truck Series during the summer of 1999. During races 11 through 19 on the schedule, Biffle won six times. He won eight times in a 12-race stretch, never going two races in a row without a victory. His ninth win of the season was his second consecutive and fourth in five events.

But Biffle's championship quest actually was hurt by his ninth win, which came at Las Vegas Motor Speedway.

Greg Biffle's truck success for Roush Racing led to a ride in the Busch Series.

Sam Sharpe

Afterwards, NASCAR officials took 120 points away from Biffle and fined his crew chief $48,860 for using an unapproved intake manifold. The penalty was the difference between 1st and 36th place, and Biffle's lead, which had been at 130 points, dropped to 10 over Sprague. "It wouldn't have been so bad if we were trying to slip something past them," Biffle says. "But we ran with it several times before, and they always approved it then. The Grainger team earned a championship. I don't want to seem like sour grapes, but these guys did what it took to win a title. They worked so hard and deserved it. We are a championship team."

Biffle still held the points lead going into the final race of the 1999 season, but he lost the title to Sprague. Interestingly, Sprague claimed that Biffle cost him the 1998 Craftsman title when the two wound up racing hard for position during the last laps of the season. Sprague won that 1998 season finale, but his battle with Biffle slowed him down enough that several other trucks bunched up behind them. Ron Hornaday won the title by passing two other trucks in the pack on the last lap.

Biffle readily admits to an error in judgment in 1998, but he wants to use 1999 as a springboard to put all previous errors behind him. He doesn't care about the sound of his voice or which part of the country he comes from. He wants to be classified as a winner.

"This has been the year of my career, almost no matter what happens in the future," Biffle says. "I've learned what it takes to win, something some people never figure out. People know who I am now, and there will be chances for me in the future that I never would have had without the nine wins in 1999. Any driver on any circuit would love to have done what I did.

"I feel so good about our chances for next year. We've learned so much, we've got it together, and we know what it takes. I'm confident we'll win a championship."

HOOKED ON RACING

BY GREG BIFFLE
From *Stock Car Racing*, July 2002

After getting "the call" that Jack Roush wanted him in his stable, Greg Biffle has won a truck series championship and two rookie-of-the-year honors. Now he hopes to drive his No. 60 Grainger Ford to a NASCAR Busch Series championship.

My story is probably a lot different than most drivers in NASCAR. I wasn't born into a racing family, and I didn't start racing at an early age running go karts or midgets with hopes of someday competing against NASCAR's elite. I wish sometimes that maybe I would've done so, but I believe things happen for a reason and this was the path chosen for me.

To be honest, in my younger days I actually thought the idea of running in circles was ridiculous. It wasn't until I was about 17 years old that I got the racing bug.

One weekend my dad and I went out to Portland Speedway in Portland, Oregon, to watch some Friday night races. Something inside me changed. I really enjoyed the competition and decided I had to take a shot at racing. My dad and I built a street stock, and I finished in the top 10 in my first race at Portland Speedway. The entire experience was like no other, and from that moment on I was hooked.

I raced on and off for a few years after that, and then I opened a business (J&S Racing) in 1990 that built and maintained NASCAR late-model cars for teams running in the Northwest region. I focused more of my attention on the business rather than actually racing for the next few years, but I believe doing that had a huge impact on the success I've had behind the wheel.

I learned so much about the mechanical aspects of the cars.

My racing career started going full steam when I won track championships at both Portland Speedway and Tri-City Raceway (West Richland, Washington). We won 16 of 24 races at Portland and 17 out of 19 at Tri-City, only to lose the national NASCAR Weekly Racing Series championship by one win.

Biffle has had a steady road to success since pairing with Roush Racing. *Nigel Kinrade*

Finally in 1997, the opportunity to race with NASCAR's elite looked a little better when Benny Parsons came to my rescue. He saw me compete in the Winter Heat Series at Tucson Raceway Park in Arizona, and I guess he saw something that others hadn't. After winning back-to-back Winter Heat championships, Benny became an advocate of mine and told every owner that they couldn't pass up on the opportunity to put me behind the wheel of one of their race cars. Still, the phone wasn't ringing.

Later that year I got a call out of the blue from Roush Racing. I was working in the shop when Geoff Smith (president of Roush Racing) told me Jack wanted me to drive for his newly formed No. 50 Craftsman Truck Series team. He hired me right there over the phone, sight unseen.

The rest is history. Jack Roush, Grainger, Randy Goss, and the guys I've worked with over the last few years have had a great deal of success. We won rookie-of-the-year honors in 1998, a record nine races in 1999, and a championship in the truck series in 2000. We jumped up to the Busch Series last year and won rookie honors again. This year we are running for the Busch championship, and then next year we're all moving up to Winston Cup together.

Looking back on my career so far, I pride myself in the things I've done because I worked hard for all of it. It's been an awesome ride and I wouldn't change a thing.

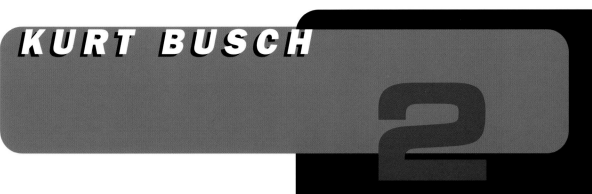

KURT BUSCH

2

Born: August 4, 1978

Hometown: Las Vegas, Nevada

Height: 5-11

Weight: 150 lbs.

Sponsor	**Rubbermaid**
Make	**Ford**
Crew Chief	**Jimmy Fennig**
Owner	**Georgetta Roush**

NASCAR Winston Cup Career Statistics

Year	Races	Wins	Top 5s	Top 10s	Poles	Total Points	Final Standing	Winnings
2000	7	0	0	0	0	613	48	$311,915
2001	35	0	3	6	1	3,081	27	$2,170,629
2002	36	4	12	20	1	4,641	3	$3,635,192
Totals	78	4	15	26	2	8,335		$6,117,736

Newell Rubbermaid and its Sharpie pen brand came on as Busch's sponsor seven races into the 2001 season, and the rookie has made the most of the company's involvement.

Harold Hinson

GROOVIN' IN GLITTER GULTCH

BY BOB MYERS
From *Circle Track,* December 2001

Kurt Busch Is One Las Vegas Export Looking to Hit the Jackpot in NASCAR's Premier Series

Jack Roush picked Busch out of a five-driver scrum for a seat in his NASCAR Craftsman Truck Series ride and then promised to take him to Winston Cup full time. *John Pyle*

What with nearly 36 million visitors annually, it seems nobody is from Las Vegas. Kurt Busch is proof, though, that not only are people actually born and raised in the world-famous oasis in the Nevada desert, but a few become professional race car drivers.

Busch has emerged as a leading newcomer to the NASCAR Winston Cup Series, not via the surreal Las Vegas Strip with its neon glitter, but on such bull-ring racetracks as Pahrump Valley Speedway and Las Vegas Speedway Park, where he cut his racing groove.

Busch, who turned 23 in August, is the second-youngest driver, next to Casey Atwood, competing full time this year in NASCAR's premier series. He's the rookie driver of the No. 97 Sharpie/Rubbermaid Ford in Roush Racing's four-team stable. Given his age and the elite organization's support and resources, Busch's future in Winston Cup appears as bright as the Vegas lights.

Compares to Gordon

Team owner Jack Roush is starry-eyed. "I wouldn't trade him for anybody I've seen," Roush says. "Obviously Tony Stewart set a really high standard as a rookie, but he was older and had more experience. Putting age in perspective, Kurt compares favorably to what I think Jeff Gordon did when he came in at 21 or 22. I think he will be able to do everything Gordon has done. That's my prediction, if I am able to support him with a team."

The first half of Busch's first full season in Winston Cup was up and down, typically rookie, even for the most talented. In the first 16 races, he logged two top 5s, three top 10s, compiled an average finish of 23rd, and ranked 23rd in championship points and second in the rookie-of-the-year standings.

There were high spots that lend credence to Roush's appraisal: 3rd place at Talladega, 4th at Texas, 10th at Atlanta, and 11th at hometown Las Vegas. Crashes in successive outings at Dover and Michigan cost him five spots in championship points.

Steep Learning Curve

Although Busch had a remarkable 2000 season with Roush in the NASCAR Craftsman Truck Series, he says Winston Cup is something else.

"The hardest adjustment is learning to drive and set up a Winston Cup car," says Busch, who has driven 10 types of racing cars and trucks in his relatively short eight-year career. "Most everything I have driven, I've adapted to rather quickly. With the Winston Cup car, there is really no pattern and the setup is different at practically every track."

Then there are the tracks. He favors wide, smooth tracks with fast lanes, such as Texas, Talladega, and California. On the flipside, "Martinsville is the toughest for me, followed by Rockingham and Darlington," says Busch, noting respective finishes of 33rd, 36th, and 30th the first time out at those foreign lands.

"The competition level of Winston Cup is unmatched, and there is no way to fully prepare for it," Busch says. "Whether you have run in the Busch Series or trucks, you have to get thrown to the sharks, like Roush has done to me."

Busch says crew chief Ben Leslie is a definite asset in helping figure out the cars. Leslie, former car chief for Roush's Matt Kenseth and crew chief for Johnny Benson for a short time, was promoted within the Roush ranks, replacing Matt Chambers, crew chief for Busch in the truck series. Leslie led Busch to the fourth place at Texas in their first race together.

"Ben brought a lot of shock knowledge to me and a lot of different ideas," Busch says. "He's very well-rounded."

Busch's team also gained primary sponsorship when Newell Rubbermaid made its debut in the Winston Cup after the seventh race. One of the company's products is the Sharpie pen, a fringe benefit Busch and most NASCAR drivers use to sign autographs. John Deere departed as the No. 97 sponsor at the end of 2000, but Roush kept his commitment to bring Busch to Winston Cup full time.

"With the crew chief change and a strong sponsor for Kurt, we're on track, looking to make the middle of the year work and hopefully to finish with a big rally," says Roush.

Product of a Program

Busch is another of a number of blue-chip rookies who've come up through top Winston Cup owners' talent scouting and driver development programs.

In fact, Busch got his break into the big time through Roush Racing auditions, dubbed *The Gong Show* after a former zany Chuck Barris TV program. After winning a televised Southwest Series race at Sears Point Raceway and the next one at Tucson in cars owned by Craig Keough and sponsored by Star Nursery of Las Vegas, Busch was selected among five finalists nationally and invited to a Roush tryout in Toledo, Ohio, in 1999.

"We drove the truck with fresh and old tires and talked with the crew chief about what adjustments we thought were needed," Busch says. "The bottom line

Kurt Busch went from truck series rookie phenom to Winston Cup rookie challenger in a scant two seasons.
Nigel Kinrade

As a truck series driver, Busch was flashy and fast. His first race, the inaugural truck race at Daytona International Speedway, served notice that he was one to watch. He won four races, finished second in the points, and was rookie of the year. *John Pyle*

was lap time—how fast we could get around the track in a given time. I didn't really think I did very well that day. I might have put too much pressure on myself, but I was fortunate to get a second chance at Phoenix International Raceway in early November. That time I knew I had done my best."

Around Thanksgiving, Geoff Smith, president of Roush Racing, informed Busch he'd gotten the job to

Busch takes his advice where he can find it, here tapping into the insights of Dale Earnhardt

Jr. *Harold Hinson*

Kurt Busch drives just like his hometown of Las Vegas—fast, flashy, and full of promise.

Harold Hinson

drive a Roush truck, effective in 2000, and he needed to relocate near Roush Industries in Michigan.

"I'm pretty well convinced the race I won at Sears Point on live TV is what attracted Jack Roush's attention and interest in me, even though I had not yet met the boss," he says.

Life-Changing Choice

Joining Roush precipitated a drastic change in Busch's pace and life. He had enjoyed a banner year on the track, winning the Southwest Series championship with six wins, including four in a row. He also finished eighth in his first Winston West race at Las Vegas Motor Speedway.

Busch left his job with the Las Vegas Valley Water District and what seemed a perfect world. Four 10-hour graveyard shifts installing and removing pipelines and repairing valves and hydrants gave him weekends off to race Southwest cars for Keough and sometimes a late model for owner Jerry Spilsbury.

Busch responded to his first year with Roush with an unparalleled rookie performance in the No. 99 Exide-sponsored Ford trucks. After opening with second at Daytona, Busch won a rookie-record four times, at Milwaukee, New Hampshire, Dover, and California, finished second in points to teammate Greg Biffle, and earned rookie-of-the-year honors. He posted 13 top 5s, 16 top 10s, had one DNF, and compiled an average finish of 8.0 in 24 starts.

"The success we had was unbelievable, something no one expected, including myself," Busch says. "The equipment was the most important element and the second was I had driven so many [different] race cars in such a short time that the truck was just another vehicle I had to conquer."

Roush was ecstatic, saying Busch was head-and-shoulders above his peers at the rate he adapted to changes on the track and to tracks he had not seen before.

But that's getting ahead of the story. In mid-June, in the midst of the truck season, Roush asked Busch to drive his Winston Cup car at Dover.

"I hadn't even won my first truck race," Busch says. "I thought he was crazy. All I could think of to say was, 'If you're ready, I'm ready.' "

Roush explains, "When John Deere was looking for a way to revitalize the No. 97 program last year, I offered Kurt as a way to really build a future program and get everybody excited about the things he was doing. He was ahead of what would be a normal schedule for a driver. They signed up for that. I made the decision to bring him up from the truck series. Then the CEO changed at John Deere and all that went upside down."

Pumped to the hilt, Busch won the next truck race at Milwaukee and the next at Dover, in addition to his Winston Cup debut, experiencing the most memorable weekends to that point of his burgeoning career. Standing in victory circle at the Milwaukee Mile, Busch looked into the grandstand at the spot where his paternal grandparents, Leonard and Joann, had sat with their son and his father, Tom, watching the races years ago. They came from the suburbs of Chicago. Busch's father had told him exactly where to look.

"My grandfather never raced and I never knew him, but he sparked my father's interest and is the reason my family got involved in racing," Busch says. "To win that race and have my grandfather's spirit there was a high point for me."

On His Way

To win the truck race at Dover, qualify his Winston Cup Ford 10th, drive almost 400 miles for the first time, and finish a respectable 18th only two laps down was a thrill almost equal to Milwaukee. After he qualified, Busch recalls the late Dale Earnhardt approaching him and saying, "Son, I didn't think you were going to lift to make that corner. You drove in too deep."

Busch was awed. He grew up watching Earnhardt and Mark Martin, his favorites, race on TV.

"It's wonderful having Mark as a teammate," Busch says. "Unfortunately, I didn't have the chance to know Earnhardt very well."

Busch competed in seven Winston Cup races last year with a best finish of 13th in the 500-miler at Charlotte. Busch wants to win a race and improve his finishes the remainder of this season, but his primary objective is to adapt to the tracks. His strong points are confidence, optimism, and smarts. His weakest point is lack of patience, which he attributes to the trials and tribulations of a big-league yearling.

Busch is striving to gain the respect of his peers.

"I had a few rough edges at first, ruffled some feathers and stepped out of bounds, coming from the truck series and wanting to go to the front," he says. "I knew how to get to the front in trucks, but I didn't know how in Winston Cup. But I've calmed down. I'm trying to show them this year I am a race car driver who wants to win but also cooperate and to be as safe as possible."

FROM HYDRANTS TO THE CUP

BY JASON MITCHELL
From *Stock Car Racing*, March 2003

An Interview with Kurt Busch

Not too long ago Kurt Busch was working for the Las Vegas Water District replacing hydrants. He may have needed a little Vegas good fortune to get his first major break in the sport, but talent has kept him moving up. Now he's out to demonstrate that he's not just a contender to win races, but a contender for a Winston Cup championship.

After picking up four wins and finishing third in Winston Cup points last year, how bad did you hate to see the 2002 season come to an end?

We were on such a serious roll at the end of last year that it did make it tough to see the season come to an end. Now we've got a lot of pressure to back up the results we had in the third quarter of 2002. To me, it's going to be fun because that will be another element I have to step up to this year.

How did you seemingly improve so much in just one year?

The biggest element was the addition of Jimmy Fennig's experience as my crew chief and me trying to step my game up to his level. It was nice having somebody like him who would listen to what I had to say and also quiz me at the same time. Over time, I feel like I would have eventually become a winning driver, but Jimmy Fennig definitely helped speed the process up a great deal.

Tell us about picking up your first Winston Cup victory in that thrilling duel with Jimmy Spencer in the spring race at Bristol.

There was just something throughout that entire race telling me it was my day. I ran into the back of somebody early in the race and had to come in the pits to fix the front of the car so it wouldn't overheat. Then the pit strategy started playing into our favor. Once I got the lead, I knew it was my race to lose. It didn't matter if somebody took the lead from me because I was going to take it back.

After the race at Bristol, Jimmy Spencer had some strong words for the way you took the lead from him. In looking back on that situation, would you do anything differently if you had the chance to replay that race?

No.

Have you learned that there are some drivers you can race side-by-side with for 20 laps and never touch while you just want to stay out of the way of others?

Absolutely. Now that I'm running up front more

Busch quickly became a contender in one of Jack Roush's Fords, winning four races in his second season. *Sam Sharpe*

> *"I believe we're going to contend for the championship this year. If we don't, we're not going to get bummed out because we know time is working in our favor."*
>
> —Kurt Busch

often, there is a lot of different camaraderie going back and forth with the drivers I'm racing against. Of course, you have the occasional run-ins with other drivers who you remember and put in the back of your mind. The next time they come up to pass you, you'll not make it as easy for them. I try to keep my focus on my car and how it's doing and not put myself in a bad situation.

How do up-and-coming drivers like yourself learn to draw the line between being young and aggressive as opposed to being tagged as disrespectful to the veterans?

It's a balancing act. The veterans are who made the sport what it is today. The first step is to build your relationship with the veterans to let them know you will race them in the manner they like to be raced against. Over time, that helps you develop into who you are and what you're about. So you do put a focus on racing the veterans cleanly, yet you still have to take care of your priorities. For me, my priority is that No. 97 car and

A win at Martinsville in 2002 had Busch smiling in victory lane. *Harold Hinson*

Busch says crew chief Jimmy Fennig (right) has shortened his learning curve. *Sam Sharpe*

You've seemed to almost come out of nowhere in your racing career, and a lot of fans haven't gotten the chance to know a lot about you personally. Away from the track, what are some things people don't know about you?

The first and foremost thing to me is my family. I love to have them at the races with me. I also try to go back to Las Vegas and visit them as often as I can or have them come to the Charlotte area where I live now. I'm also a big pet lover. I have a dog I call Jim that travels with me everywhere I go. As a kid, I used to tinker with radio-controlled cars. I still enjoy racing those things. I always take them on the road with me, so when qualifying or practice is over, that's what I do to relax. A lot of the time when we're on the road, me and some of my buddies will go find an R/C track to race at somewhere.

Did you grow up wanting to become a Winston Cup driver or was another career path ever considered?

I was a realistic guy who looked at things in a view of what I could accomplish. I knew I had to graduate from high school with good enough grades to get into college because I wanted to pursue a degree in pharmaceuticals. I wanted to have my own little pharmacy one day in a small retirement town. I was also hoping that small town had a racetrack so I could race on Friday or Saturday nights.

How did you first get interested in racing?

I used to spend a lot of time at the old Craig Road Speedway (in Las Vegas), where my dad started racing street stocks the year I was born. It was just a little quarter-mile oval, and they would have big money races at the end of the year. You'd see guys come in there like Alan Kulwicki, Dick Trickle, Rusty Wallace, and Mark Martin. That's where my dad raced, so I spent a lot of my Saturday nights there while I was growing up. During the week I'd spend all my time in the garage with my dad tinkering on his race cars.

Didn't you work at the Las Vegas Water District to earn extra spending money so you could race on the weekends?

I sure did. It started out as a summer internship, and I worked on the distribution crew. We did construction and replaced old service lines. We would replace fire hydrants some days and go out other days to fix the water lines that led to houses. It was pretty much just a lot of different kinds of construction. Then I moved to the graveyard shift and was making some pretty good money, plus the hours worked out pretty good for a young guy growing up in Las Vegas. I'd work four 10-hour days, then have Friday through Sunday off so I could spend my weekends racing.

At age 21 you became the youngest champion to win the NASCAR Featherlite Southwest Series title. A lot of young talent wants to make it to the Winston Cup level, but did that goal seem like something that was a million miles away from reality back in those days?

At that point in time, of course it did. The way things have progressed with my career so quickly in meeting the right people and being in the right places at the right time has been unreal. I was aware that I was being looked at

keeping all my sponsors happy. You have to give the veterans a lot of respect because of what they've done for the history of this sport. It's a unique balance for a young driver, treading lightly through the waters.

What's the biggest mistake you've made since becoming a Winston Cup regular?

Just being a little bit overly aggressive and trying to do too many things that were out of my control. At Indianapolis last year I felt like my life was at stake, and I was deemed wrong for the end result. I just have to look back on stuff like that and learn from it. After I got wrecked, I was sitting in the driver's seat with all this adrenaline running through me, and I knew I'd been done wrong. There are other ways to handle that than the way I did when I got out of the car.

If you had only one or two words to describe your driving style, what would it be?

I've never really sat down and thought about how to describe myself. I guess one word would be *determined*; another word would be *hungry*.

Busch has shown he's not afraid to bend up a little sheet metal to get to the front, as was obvious following his win at Martinsville. *Harold Hinson*

by the Roush organization when I won the Southwest Tour championship, but I had no idea where it was going to lead. I thought they were considering starting up a Southwest Tour team and looking for a driver. In the back of my mind there was the reality of them not hiring me, so I was also lining up other things on the side just in case things didn't work out.

I know you have a 17-year-old brother, Kyle, whose been showing a lot of potential in trying to follow in your racing footsteps. Where does his career stand now and how much do you try to help him along?

That poor kid has been through so many age limit restrictions scenarios it's ridiculous. Kyle has kept a level head about it because he knows he has plenty of time. He has been learning as much about racing as he can. He's had my dad's help and now he has my help. Hopefully, Kyle will be able to make it into the truck series when he does turn 18 in May. We're working on a contract with the folks at Roush Racing, but he really can't sign anything until his birthday.

So who's the better driver, Kurt or Kyle Busch?

Kyle legitimately beat me once in a Legend's car race back in 1999 when I was running for the Southwest Tour championship. It was an off weekend when we raced, and I just couldn't get past him. We both started in the back, and he made it to the front quicker than I did. I was taking the turtle approach, but the hare beat me that day.

You've had a lot happen in your life in a short time span. In five years you've gone from a virtual unknown driver with a dream to a legitimate threat to win the Winston Cup championship. How have you been able to manage so much quick success?

I've been through such a quick rise through all the different levels of racing it really has been somewhat mind-boggling and hard to grasp everything. There are a lot of different things that Winston Cup drivers go through both on and off the track that consume a great deal of time. Your old friends become a little more distant, and you have a new family that is the racing community.

What are some of the things that you've tried not to lose sight of?

Not losing focus of how much credibility a driver can have with his race team. I might put myself in a situation where I'm too accessible to my team, but I want them to feel like I'm just one of them. I believe that we as a team are in this together, whether it's the guys in the fabrication shop or the crew during the race. I want them to know I can't do this without them. So that's been something I've tried to do, and it's not just something I do and don't mean. I enjoy the camaraderie, and it's seemed to be a morale boost to the team.

As far as the No. 97 team, what will constitute a good 2003 season, and did you and your team set certain goals over the winter?

We want to continue our strong effort of running up front so we can create a situation where we can be in contention for the championship. That's going to take a great deal of consistency and finishing races. If we can chop the number of races we don't finish in half compared to last year, I really feel like we can compete for the championship.

We've talked about all the success you had last year, but in the back of your mind is there a fear of letdown if you guys don't go out and win another four races and finish third or better in points this season?

It would be the first time I've ever gone the wrong direction. I think the bottom line is you always are supposed to do better than the year before because you have more experience. I'm not really worried about living up to what we did last year, but if we didn't I would want to know why. I feel like I've got time on my side and a great relationship with both Jack Roush and Jimmy Fennig. I believe we're going to contend for the championship this year. If we don't, we're not going to get bummed out because we know time is working in our favor.

" . . . I wanted to pursue a degree in pharmaceuticals. I wanted to have my own little pharmacy one day in a small retirement town."

—Kurt Busch

Busch says he respects veteran drivers, but his top priority is the No. 97 Rubbermaid Ford.

Sam Sharpe

DALE EARNHARDT JR.

3

Born: October 10, 1974

Hometown: Kannapolis, North Carolina

Height: 6-0

Weight: 165 lbs.

Sponsor	**Budweiser**
Make	**Chevrolet**
Crew Chief	**Tony Eury Sr.**
Owner	**Teresa Earnhardt**

NASCAR Winston Cup Career Statistics

Year	Races	Wins	Top 5s	Top 10s	Poles	Total Points	Final Standing	Winnings
1999	5	0	0	1	0	500	48	$162,095
2000	34	2	3	5	2	3,516	16	$2,801,880
2001	36	3	9	15	2	4,460	8	$5,827,542
2002	36	2	11	16	2	4,270	11	$4,305,021
Totals	111	7	23	37	6	12,746		$13,096,538

Dale Earnhardt Jr.'s success in the Busch Series made him the most promising young star since Jeff Gordon. *Nigel Kinrade*

LITTLE E MAKES
THE BIG TIME

BY BOB MYERS
From *Circle Track* February 1999

Budweiser Takes a Risk in Making

the Biggest Deal in NASCAR History

With Earnhardt Jr. at the wheel, an already competitive Busch team became a championship team. *Nigel Kinrade*

You knew it was a big deal, this first official function at Dale Earnhardt Incorporated's (DEI) new "Garage Mahal."

Inside what looked more like a ballroom than part of a 133,000-square-foot race shop, there were uniformed caterers and tables of fancy hors d'oeuvres. There were car-parkers outside in the rain and pretty girls in red shirts directing guests along corridors to the press conference. Dale Earnhardt had done many things in racing, but hosting a press conference was a first—this time as a father and car owner.

A few of us who have covered Earnhardt throughout his long driving career couldn't help but reflect on the seven-time Winston Cup champion's humble start, which was in his racing father Ralph's two-bay garage with one race car at their modest home in Kannapolis, North Carolina. Talent and determination far exceeded money. Racing became a struggle for Earnhardt after his father, as good a short-track driver as there ever was, died unexpectedly. A dream has mushroomed into benchmark accomplishments

and millions of dollars in earnings, much of which has been plowed back into the first-class operation and ownership of three race teams with 114 employees.

On this day, though, some 25 years later, 23-year-old Dale Earnhardt Jr. made his grand entrance riding shotgun on the Budweiser wagon drawn by several tons of horsepower—eight Clydesdales. All this was fit for the king of beers and the would-be prince of stock car racing. Oh, only if Ralph Earnhardt, could see his son and grandson now.

The deal was much bigger than most in the room could imagine. Anheuser-Busch had signed Dale Earnhardt Jr. and DEI to a six-year contract to tout its premier brand, Budweiser, in the Winston Cup Series beginning in 1999. Junior will compete in five selected Winston Cup races for Budweiser next year, while driving his second full season in the Busch Grand National Series. He'll then tackle the big circuit full time in 2000. His 1999 schedule and car number will be announced later.

Although the price tag was removed from the sponsorship and personal services package, an educated guess places the value as high as $60 million. Wow! Is this NASCAR or professional baseball? Given that Winston Cup agreements are normally three years, this has to be the biggest team sponsorship outlay in NASCAR history.

DEI President Don Hawk declined to divulge the figure, but he says, "I believe if everybody is telling their true numbers, this is one of the biggest deals in Winston Cup, including Dale Sr.'s [with GM Goodwrench and Richard Childress Racing] and Jeff Gordon's [with DuPont and Hendrick Motorsports]. And I'm not talking about endorsements. Dale Sr. already had an endorsement agreement with Budweiser. I will also say that no one company handed no one person $10 million per year, but Anheuser-Busch's agreement with Dale Jr., in racing language, is really stout."

Risky Business

There are sound reasons why Anheuser-Busch would risk millions on a rookie driver who had not even driven a Winston Cup car in competition at the time of the agreement. Obviously, based on Little E.'s first full Busch season, he has the Earnhardt racing genes and is considered the best prospect since Gordon appeared in 1993 and took the series by storm. Through 27 races, Earnhardt Jr. led the Busch Series, NASCAR's triple-A league, in most performance categories, with six victories, three poles, 14 top 5s, 20 top 10s, earnings of $718,000, and a 97-point lead toward his first championship. Not bad for a youngster who had competed previously in only a dozen Busch races. By comparison, Jeff Gordon, the current Winston Cup rage, won three Busch Grand National races, 12 poles, had 13 top 5s, 23 top 10s, and $519,000 in earnings in 62 starts over two seasons.

Additionally, Budweiser has been associated with Big E for many years, more closely over the past five, and knows his illustrious record and his passion for excellence. Also, it was a matter of opportunity and timing.

Dale Jr. had planned to join Winston Cup in 2000 and Budweiser, the country's leader in money spent on sports advertising, was looking for another team to sponsor. The company has gotten very little positive exposure from the winless Hendrick Motorsports team it backs, but it will continue to sponsor that team and driver Wally Dallenbach for the 1999 season.

It has been a whirlwind year for Little E, what with things happening so fast. "Our Busch team was a winner when I became the driver and now it's a championship contender," Dale Jr. says. "Maybe we were lucky in that we've done so well. That allowed us to think about new opportunities. Budweiser was ready to make an agreement and was interested in me and my program. A year ago, I never thought I'd be driving a Winston Cup car prepared on this scale and sponsored by one of the most prestigious companies in all of sport. I'm not real surprised at our Busch team's success, but I am amazed and thrilled at getting Budweiser."

Dale Jr. is having to adjust to the series of events in his life, but not too much. "I want to continue to be myself and do the things I want to do," he says. "I'm just taking things as they come and trying not to be overwhelmed." Little E says being himself means living in a mobile home across the highway from the Garage Mahal near Mooresville, North Carolina. "That's me and it keeps me sane," he adds.

He can now expect to live in a fish bowl and the trailer to turn to glass.

Budweiser is convinced Dale Jr. is a blue blood. "Dale Jr. has demonstrated he has the ability to become the next star in Winston Cup," says August Busch IV, Anheuser-Busch's vice president of marketing. But Dale Jr. will be a rookie, and still the deal is a multi-million-dollar gamble for Budweiser if Little E falls below expectations. Patience is a key word here.

Life in the Big Leagues

Practically all rookies hit a literal and figurative wall when they advance to the big league, which is a giant leap from Busch. Rookies in 1998, Steve Park, who drives for the Winston Cup team Dale Sr. owns; Kevin Lepage; Kenny Irwin; and Jerry Nadeau were a testimony to that fact. Park missed 14 races with injuries. The highly billed Irwin had one top five and ranked 28th in points after 29 races. Lepage, 35th in points, quit his ride and signed on with Jack Roush, and Nadeau, 36th in points, changed rides.

There are former Busch champions who haven't won in four or five years in Winston Cup. Even Jeff Gordon was winless his rookie year before he took off in 1994. In fact, only five rookies of the year since 1958 have won a race, and Dale Sr. is one of them.

Perhaps Little E will be the exception after a taste of Winston Cup competition and another full season of Busch.

"I'm not going to neglect the fact that everybody is taking a risk here," says Dale Jr. "That's obvious. I don't have that much experience, but I think I know what I'm doing and think I am capable of doing the job Budweiser [and his daddy] wants. If I didn't think I've proved myself, I'd be a lot more worried about the situation. Deals like this are like investing in the stock market. Will it go up or down?" Dale Jr. is convinced he and his team can make the transition from Busch to Winston Cup together and be competitive.

Dale Jr. bears a physical resemblance to his daddy, expresses himself pretty well, and isn't as shy as Big E. He seems to be a nice kid. But Dale Jr. is the

Like his famous father, Earnhardt Jr. prefers an open-face helmet. *Nigel Kinrade*

Away from his car and out of his driving uniform, Earnhardt Jr. looks like any other young southern man. *Nigel Kinrade*

Earnhardt Jr. doing what an Earnhardt does best, taking control of a race car. *Nigel Kinrade*

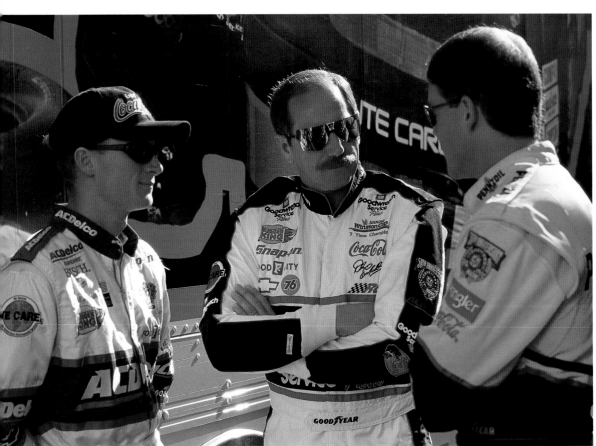

The Earnhardts and DEI driver Steve Park (far right). *Nigel Kinrade*

car and you're aggressive, it's hard to back that thing down a little and stay out of trouble. One lesson I learned from my father when I was a kid is that you can take a driver who drives the car over his head and wrecks nearly every race and calm him down and pull him back a notch and make him a winner. You can't do that with a driver who won't drive the car hard, especially into the corners. Dale Jr. will drive the car. We've got to harness and detune him, and he'll be a winner. I am very proud of him and what he has done in the Busch Series. I'm proud of all my [four] kids." Big E's older son, Kerry, advances to Busch next year.

"As a parent, you always want the best for your children," adds Earnhardt Sr., "and that's what we're doing for Dale Jr. and his career. Budweiser's support guarantees he'll be starting in Winston Cup with the best of everything.

"As a driver, though, he's one more of these young guns I'll have to beat."

Earnhardt Sr., 47, whose black No. 3 Childress Racing Chevrolet is almost as famous as Richard Petty's No. 43, has driven around the world almost eight times—more than 194,000 miles—in more than 600 Winston Cup starts dating to 1975 and has won about everything the sport offers. Even though he rebounded from a winless 1997 season to victory in the Daytona 500, he and his team have slipped inexplicably into what is mediocrity for them. He has tried four times unsuccessfully to win a record eighth championship. Earnhardt's loyal fans have had little to cheer about, though they've embraced Little E. They have been occupied, however, booing the feats of Jeff Gordon.

Earnhardt is not ready to pass the torch to his son, but that may come sooner than expected if his performance doesn't return to a high level. "My performance and that of the team together, I think, will be a major factor in determining how long I drive," Earnhardt says. "I feel comfortable racing through the year 2000, when my contract with Childress is up, maybe beyond.

"I don't know how I'll feel in two years, whether I want to race past 50. We'll have to wait and see. I don't like the way we've been racing, whether the problem is part team or part driver. I want to be the car to beat. Right now we're not that kind of force in Winston Cup and we've got to get back to that position. I want to win by beating the best or run second and get beat by the best. I want to quit driving on my own terms and avoid a situation where people write me off." Some people think that now but wouldn't dare say it.

Earnhardt won't drive for himself. "I don't like myself that good," he says, adding levity. "And I don't want to argue with my wife [Teresa] about her car or my driving. I can argue with Richard Childress, not her, because I'd lose."

Big E wants to remain a part of the NASCAR family as a car owner for many years. He's busy preparing for that day.

1979 image of his father in a race car—very aggressive. Well, he was. Excellent coaching by his daddy and crew chief Tony Eury Sr. has reeled in Little Intimidator.

"I think Dale Jr. will be OK," says Big E. "He is using his head and racing much smarter. He's shown a lot of poise and was ready to do what it takes to win. That's hard to do. When you've got a good race

THE MULTIMILLION-DOLLAR MAN

BY BOB MYERS
From *Circle Track*, October 1999

Earnhardt Jr. started 8th and finished 16th in his Winston Cup debut at Charlotte. *Nigel Kinrade*

Old-timers say Dale Earnhardt Jr. has received more attention and hype than any other rookie debuting in Winston Cup. There were press conferences here and teleconferences there and appearances elsewhere. A gaggle of media shadowed him at the track, actually taking some of the pressure off Jeff Gordon. Outgoing, talkative, accommodating, and as yet unspoiled, Little E handled the crunch like a pro.

Why such fanfare for a rookie? Well, not all rookies are named Earnhardt. Not all rookies win the Busch Series championship their first year. Not all rookies have a six-year contract estimated at $60 million with Budweiser, a blend of the prince and king. Not all rookies have a built-in army of fans amassed by his daddy. Not all rookies rank third in souvenir sales behind his dad and Jeff Gordon. Not all rookies have made more money in four months than in the preceding 23 years.

Earnhardt's very respectable 8th start and 16th finish in the 600 took the anvil off his shoulders in relief and satisfaction. His worries about pleasing everybody, especially Big E, were allayed. Dad was pleased, though his highest compliment was "good job." After all, Big E had started 33rd and finished 22nd in his Winston Cup debut at the same speedway in the 1975 600.

"I just tried not to make a fool of myself and tear up my car," says Little E. "I hope the Winston Cup drivers feel more comfortable around me—that's the one thing I was trying to accomplish. I tried to learn as much as I could by following the other cars. It was what I expected. Those guys are true professionals. I was awed by what they can do and the places they can go with a race car. I am pleased with most aspects of the first race. After we finished second in the Busch race and qualified well for the 600, I raised expectations from a top-20 finish to a top 10, but we're not even close to being ready for that." He gave himself a "C." Four more races are to follow this season.

Junior didn't reveal his biggest concern—endurance—until after the fact, however. He had not raced 500 miles, much less 600. "I didn't get worn out, but I got all sorts of aches and pains in my neck and back. My fitness program has been ordering pizza and Budweiser. I'm going to change that and get on a treadmill. As much as I don't want to admit it, my daddy was right."

ROOKIE REPORT 2000

BY DALE EARNHARDT JR.
From *Circle Track* May 2000

Two-Time Busch Grand National Champion

Dale Earnhardt Jr. Discusses Where He's

Been and Where He's Going

Earnhardt Jr. was just beginning to realize true fame in 2000. *CT Archives*

Winning the Busch Grand National Championship in 1998 and 1999 has raised a lot of expectations about what I can do in the Winston Cup Series this year. Obviously, I want to do well, but I'm being careful not to set too many lofty goals with X-number of top 5s and top 10s. Instead, I'm going to concentrate more on running where the car is capable of running. When I was racing in the Busch Grand National Series, we never set too many of those types of goals. After awhile, I knew I could win a championship if I worked hard at it, but I didn't really say how many races I wanted to win or how well I wanted to do. We receive a large amount of pressure from a lot of areas, so that just continues to add to it.

Like I said, I tend to measure success based on finishing where the car is capable of running in relation to the rest of the field. In one of the five Winston Cup races I entered in 1999, we ran 10th at Richmond. I was really happy with that finish because I felt like that car was a 10th-place car, and I felt like, as a driver and a person, I did as good as I possibly could. At Atlanta that same year, in the Cup car, I finished 14th, but I made a mistake in the pits, so we should have finished higher. I was disappointed.

Overall, I try to take things one day at a time. In a sport where you have to continually push yourself harder all the time, I've found that the less pressure I put on myself, the better I feel like I can perform. I just look at each task and each challenge, single it out, and try to accomplish it. We go to each racetrack and try to do the best we can each week. A key factor for me is the people around me. From one end of the spectrum to the other, I've got good people who are knowledgeable and know they are doing a good job and doing their job. The driver can't make a great team and make all the changes himself. During my first year in the Busch Series, I didn't know diddly about good fitness and won a championship while I was relatively inexperienced. That's due to having the right people. In order to succeed, I think you need to have a lot of respect for yourself, know your ability, and have a lot of confidence. But be reserved about it.

I really consider myself to be a normal, down-to-earth guy, but some things really hit home, like having cardboard stand-ups in convenience stores and cans of Budweiser with my name on the side. It's kind of fun. It really hits home when I walk into the convenience store down the street from the house and see the stand-up of myself in there. Then my buddies mess with me about it and make jokes like, "Man, yesterday I saw you in the convenience store downtown and ..." Well, you can fill in the rest of that sentence with whatever you like.

I pay a lot of attention to what the public thinks. Even if you are winning races, if you're not getting a positive reaction from the people who are watching, I don't feel like you're getting anywhere. I try to become a better person by continuously paying attention to the right things to do versus the wrong things to do.

The Competition

This year, my rookie year in the Winston Cup Series, has shaped up to be one of the most competitive seasons for a new class of rookies. I've read here and there that Matt Kenseth is a favorite of many people to win the rookie title. I think it's up for grabs among the entire class, but I do think it will be fairly close between Matt, Dave Blaney, and myself.

Bill France Jr. (center) and Dale Earnhardt Sr. were on hand when Junior won his second Busch title in 1999.

Nigel Kinrade

Dad and Me

Racing against Dale, my dad, is going to be pretty exciting. This column was turned in before the 2000 season even started, so maybe we've already had some good races. Over the past three years, he's kind of changed his outlook a little bit and has become even more serious about racing and his career. It's improved his performance level a bit. In the past five races from 1999, we ran around each other quite a bit, and it was enjoyable.

As for the rest of the Winston Cup field, those guys are smart and quick. At Atlanta in 1999, those guys were running right against the wall and in places that I never considered running in the Busch car. It kind of freaks you out how those guys are able to find a new groove so fast. And it's the ones you least expect, like Michael Waltrip and Jimmy Spencer, who are the guys to be thinking first. You'd expect somebody like Mark Martin or Dale Jarrett would figure out

a track's changing line faster, but it seems like those other guys do it first. You watch—Michael Waltrip is always the first person to figure out that the top groove is the fastest once the track starts to change.

The first half of the 2000 season will be a lot of work. It's probably going to take about 10 or 15 races to get a lot of confidence in myself. That includes communicating better with Tony Eury Sr. about the changes on the car.

Earnhardt Jr. expected the rookie of the year battle to be close. He was edged out by Matt Kenseth. *Harold Hinson*

EMOTIONS RUN WILD FOR EARNHARDT JR.

BY XENA ELICH
From *Circle Track,* November 2001

Pepsi 400 Victory Nearly Too Good to Be True

Dale Earnhardt Jr. dominated at Daytona and won the Pepsi 400 in dramatic fashion. The fact is that no one in Hollywood (or Daytona) could have written a better script. After he returned for the first time to the legendary track where his father was killed only five months before, many would applaud Dale Jr. for strapping in at all.

When the Budweiser-backed car crossed the finish line a scant .123 seconds ahead of Dale Earnhardt Inc. teammate Michael Waltrip, a collective chill ran down the spines of most who witnessed the event.

"Y'all know who that's for guys," Earnhardt Jr. said to his crew over his in-car radio after the victory.

Dale Jr. led 116 of 160 laps but had to charge to the finish from sixth place with six laps to go. Luckily for the Budweiser Chevrolet team, no one had a strong enough car to stay in front of Dale Jr., and he was able to make his way to the front with relative ease. He also got more than a little help from Waltrip, who ran interference for Dale Jr. down the stretch.

"Michael came in there the last two laps, and I knew I didn't have a whole lot to worry about," Earnhardt says.

Earnhardt Jr., who won for the first time this season and the third time in his Winston Cup career, clearly had the fastest car.

"We had a great car. It was all car, 100 percent. I just had to hold on," Earnhardt Jr. says, referring to the job his crew chief, Tony Eury, had done.

In what has been an emotionally charged year for NASCAR, this race did not disappoint the 170,000 spectators still mourning the loss of superstar Dale Earnhardt.

"He was with me tonight," Dale Jr. says. "I don't know how I did it. This is an awesome night. I dedicate this win to him."

In Hollywood fashion, Dale Earnhardt Jr. went back to Daytona to win the Pepsi 400 and dedicate the victory to his late father. *Nigel Kinrade*

The July race at Daytona in 2001 was the first race run at the track in over 20 years without **Dale Earnhardt Sr.** *Sam Sharpe*

Earnhardt Jr. flashed true Earnhardt form in taking the Daytona victory. *Nigel Kinrade*

ON THE ROAD WITH JUNIOR

BY LARRY COTHREN
From *Stock Car Racing*, June 2002

NASCAR's Emerging Superstar Seeks Balance—and Victories—in His Life

It's the day after Christmas and Dale Earnhardt Jr. and three friends embark on a road trip—one of those journeys you take when you're 27, wealthy, single, and anxious to kick around for a few days.

Another friend, a 21-year-old aspiring racer, is ready to make a career move, relocating from Buffalo to the Charlotte area, and Junior and company head north in a red truck borrowed from Dale Earnhardt Chevrolet. They'll lend a hand to their New York buddy and live it up a little before they return to North Carolina.

"We got just past Greensboro [North Carolina] and turned off the interstate and just followed the compass from there on out, never got on another four-lane road," says Earnhardt. "It was pretty cool going through all those back roads. We went to Washington, D.C., and took our picture in front of the White House and in front of several of the monuments. We went through Gettysburg, Pennsylvania, and saw the battlefields, but it was about two in the morning so it was kind of hard to see what was going on. We had a good time, just kind of messed around. It took us 22 hours to get up there because we were fiddling around all day and all night."

Road trips have become prized therapy for Earnhardt, mainly because they're not at all complicated. He and some buddies will simply hop into a car and drive somewhere. Usually they'll head to a place that doesn't have a local racetrack and—here's the key—where the locals don't follow racing. It's not so much what the trips offer as what they don't offer: no public appearances to worry about, no strict schedules to adhere to, no one in your face all the time wanting you to do this or that or go there. "It's been more fun and beneficial for me when I do get time off to get totally away from it, to just go

somewhere and get out of my element altogether," says Earnhardt.

So on the way back from Buffalo the week after Christmas, Earnhardt and his buddies detour a little west, going through Ohio. Not exactly a place to get away from racing, given the 50 or so racetracks that dot the Ohio landscape, but a diversion nonetheless.

"We stopped at a bar and spent the night and had a good time," Earnhardt says. "It was a lot of fun. It was kind of cool just to get away and be normal for a while. That was definitely a reality check to get you pumped up about the year and get you back into life."

Eye of the Storm

Taking a road trip and relaxing is one of those requisite life functions when you're suddenly the face of an entire sport and the whole world wants a piece of your time. Or when

Earnhardt Jr. has quickly become one of the most recognizable people in sports. *Harold Hinson*

A media swarm usually accompanies Earnhardt Jr. at the track. *Harold Hinson*

your new book, *Driver #8*, is on the New York Times bestseller list.

If we peep into Earnhardt's life for a glimpse of how hectic and demanding it is to always be in the public eye, then it's easy to see why something so innocent as a road trip, nothing more than an escape into a life resembling normalcy, is so valuable.

Earnhardt's sister, Kelley, and his publicist, Jade Gurss, are charged with the task of making sense and order of Earnhardt's professional life.

"It's like a big, giant jigsaw puzzle," says Gurss, who co-authored *Driver #8*. "You have a lot of pieces that are strewn all over the place and the challenge is to get them to fit in the best way possible. If he were to do all of the interviews or all of the appearances that are requested, he would be working 24 hours, seven days a week. In the 10 days at Daytona, he did almost 95 interviews and nearly a dozen different sponsor appearances or functions, plus one massive autograph session for his new book." This whirlwind of attention has surrounded Earnhardt since he took the Busch Series by storm and won back-to-back

titles in 1998 and 1999. Since moving up to Winston Cup in 2000, when he promptly won two races and two poles, the intensity has increased as Earnhardt has almost single-handedly redefined stock car stardom, standing before people in places previously outside the NASCAR reach.

"We've been in a unique situation to go to different places and show people a little bit about NASCAR," says Earnhardt. "I might not represent the average mold for a NASCAR driver, but we were able to go to certain areas and certain people throughout the country, especially toward the West Coast last year, with some of the articles and some of the networks we worked with, and showed ourselves and our sport to some interesting groups of people."

Bringing Them In

It may seem odd that Dale Earnhardt Jr., with five wins in his first two Winston Cup seasons and a driver defined more by what he hasn't done on the track than what he has done, is the guy leading the NASCAR charge into new and mostly uncharted territory. It hasn't been

In his third year of Winston Cup competition, Earnhardt Jr. was still seeking a breakout season.
Harold Hinson

"The pressure is on him to continue to dazzle people with his image, his youth image, but he's got to deliver on the racetrack to keep that flame burning as strong as it is."

—Humpy Wheeler

Nontraditional motorsports sponsors have sought to be associated with Earnhardt Jr. *Sam Sharpe*

A company usually gets a lot of bang for its buck as one of Earnhardt Jr.'s sponsors. *Harold Hinson*

that long ago when he was running late models at Myrtle Beach, South Carolina. Now he's the face of the sport. Does that sound right?

Nearly all of the sporting press, and some on the outside looking in, think so. Look around and the guy is everywhere: magazine covers, profiles, everywhere a story. Not to mention appearances on MTV and *The Tonight Show* with Jay Leno, stories in *People* and *Rolling Stone*, an interview in *Playboy*—the list goes on. This is definitely not his daddy's NASCAR, and that's the whole point.

Could it be that Dale Earnhardt Jr., the man of the hour in U.S. motorsports, is just the guy to stand before an entire country and represent stock car racing? He meets all the requirements.

NASCAR has long been about lineage and heritage and many of the things in society that speak family—from American-made automobiles to children hoisted high in victory lane. NASCAR remains to this day a family-run business, one born more than 50 years ago in the South and raised on traditional southern values of hard work, loyalty, and dedication. So who better to represent the sport than a third-generation driver who is the son of the man who personified the very soul of stock car racing?

If Earnhardt Jr.'s bloodline alone is not enough to justify his place in the sport, consider this: The NASCAR growth curve demanded a younger audience, some maintain, and Earnhardt Jr. has met and exceeded the demand, and that alone has set him apart from those who've gone before him.

Humpy Wheeler, the Speedway Motorsports president who is a respected observer of the sport, says the timing was right for Earnhardt to make his mark.

"I think the pop culture that they introduced him to—or he introduced them to, that's debatable there—that's the first time that has happened, and I think it signifies the broader market we have today

compared to even five years ago, particularly the youth market," says Wheeler.

"A decade ago we were beginning to be concerned that our demographics were reaching up too high as far as age was concerned. But Jeff Gordon, as he started winning, began to change that. Now Gordon is 30 and along comes Earnhardt Jr. at the right time with the right kind of personality. He's bringing that youth group along. It's just extraordinary how the demographics of this whole business are changing even as we speak."

It's not just teenagers and twentysomethings who count themselves among the Earnhardt Jr. legion, though. Watch nearly an entire grandstand rise to its feet whenever Junior turns in a hot qualifying lap or makes a charge into the lead of a race and you'll see a cross section of fans. He can bring that young person into the NASCAR fold, but he'll also grab the loyalty of that young person's father and grandfather. Some of those fans come from his father, no doubt, but they're in the fold either way.

Another factor in Junior's ascension to the top of the sport is his ability to be himself. It's an old battle cry, but it remains a relevant one: A sport built on colorful characters lacks color today. And NASCAR drivers have long been poked fun at for their willingness to walk the walk and talk the talk to appease image-conscious sponsors. Then along comes Earnhardt Jr. with his laid-back personality, dash of color, and air of genuineness.

"I've been hearing a lot of talk about representing the sport and whether I would be one of those guys to do that or not, and maybe that's why I pressure myself on wearing just normal clothes every day and being myself," says Earnhardt. "I get a lot of flack from my sponsor for not having their logo all over my back and my shoulders and my head. Walking around in a pair of Adidas is pretty cool to me, and I want people

Earnhardt Jr.'s on-track performance will be the ultimate gauge of his success. *Sam Sharpe*

There were glitches along the way, but Earnhardt Jr. had two Busch Series titles and five Winston Cup wins by his 2002 season. *Harold Hinson*

to know that's who I am. And if you don't mind that guy who represents the sport wearing Adidas and the hat backwards, then that's fine. But if you do mind, then look somewhere else.

"You can't fool the public. When you dress somebody up and they do the dance, I think the public can tell the difference between somebody who's sincere and somebody who's not. Although I'm very proud of my relationship with all my sponsors—whether it be Budweiser or Drakkar or whoever—I don't feel like it's that necessary to don their logos everywhere I go. For some reason I think we can go further just being ourselves, and I think people will be more interested in that than billboarding."

Seeking Balance

At 27 Earnhardt Jr. is firmly established in the sport at the same age his father was as a rookie. Junior epitomizes NASCAR cool while his father at 27 was a throwback to the sport's rough-hewn past. Where Earnhardt Sr.'s trademark was a bushy mustache, Junior's trademark is a ball cap worn backwards. Yet there's a mellow, somewhat domesticated nature that reveals itself, despite the road trips—or rather because of the road trips and the balance they lend to his life. Last year he even shut down "Club E," the basement nightclub at his house. No, he's not married yet, although he has said a wife and a son would go a long way toward leading a full life. But there's only so much you can pack into a life like the one he's lived the last few years.

"For the most part, it's been a lot of fun," says Earnhardt. "Even the really heavy structure,

when it gets to be like we're doing something every day, it's still fun. There was a point last year and the year before that, every once in awhile, where you seem to kind of lose touch with your home life and your family and your friends.

This year I'm going to try to be a little more related toward that end of it, to be more involved with my friends and family than I was last year and spend some more time around them and try to get what I want out of my professional life and social life. We've been so busy running around and everything over the last couple of years that it's been really hard to maintain good relationships with my family and my friends. I'll try to do a little better with that this year.

"My mother moved from Norfolk [Virginia] about a year ago. I can just drive two miles down the road and see her, and that's really great. My sister [Kelley] had Carson, my little niece, about a year and a half ago, and that's been a lot of fun to be around her. Those things like that have made a lot of difference."

The specter of who he is and where he's going in his chosen profession is never far away, though. Ultimately, he realizes success will be gauged solely by his performance on the track. "There are all kinds of things that I want to do, and I know that to be able to do [those things] I'll have to continue as a race car driver and be good at it," he says.

There are also the inevitable questions about goals and motivation that young, rich athletes face. Earnhardt fields questions about the importance of a breakout season with reference to a couple of drivers who reached the sport's pinnacle. "It's pretty important to me,"

Earnhardt Jr. has cultivated his own distinctive look. *Nigel Kinrade*

Since getting his first Winston Cup win at Texas in 2000, Earnhardt Jr. has steadily become a leader in the sport. *Harold Hinson*

Junior looks things over in a rare free moment at the track. *Sam Sharpe*

he says. "I would say it's as important as it was to my father. If there's a gauge to go off of, I believe it would be just as important to me as it was to him or to Jeff Gordon or anybody else."

Wheeler has developed a theory on stardom and its place in NASCAR. During his five decades of involvement in stock car racing and from observing sports in general, he maintains that NASCAR got to where it is today by consistently having two superstars. The same formula

applies to other sports, according to Wheeler. Since Dale Earnhardt Sr.'s fatal crash a year and a half ago, Jeff Gordon stands as the sport's only true superstar, Wheeler maintains, and for Earnhardt Jr. to claim a spot alongside Gordon, he'll have to win more often.

"In this type of racing, to really be a superstar you've got to be a prolific winner," Wheeler says. "You can act like a superstar, you can look like a superstar, and just that charisma, those elements right there, will vault you up where everybody can see you. But you can't stay there unless you win races. So the pressure is on him to continue to dazzle people with his image, his youth image, but he's got to deliver on the racetrack to keep that flame burning as strong as it is.

"If he wins two or three races a year and we have the type of parity we have now, he might just be able to keep that going and might emerge as that second superstar."

For now, Earnhardt says his spot at the top of the sport, the spot that holds superstardom, will have to wait.

"I think," says Earnhardt, "that I will establish that a little more once we win some more races and maybe get closer to winning a championship. Right now we're just kind of growing."

Yet if we look out on the NASCAR horizon, we'll spot Earnhardt Jr. He'll be easy to pick out and not just because of his hat turned the wrong way. He'll be the one with road trips to make, family to embrace, friendships to nurture, races to win. The key to being a superstar, after all, might be the ability to live with superstardom.

WIDE-OPEN WONDERS

BY LARRY COTHREN
From *Stock Car Racing*, March 2003

Dale Earnhardt Inc. Makes Its Mark
by Dominating Restrictor-Plate Races

In NASCAR Winston Cup racing, where 18 different drivers reached victory lane last season and 19 the year before, there's still room for a little old-fashioned domination—the type that used to define the sport.

With all respect to the parity that marks big-league stock car racing, one fact stands out: Dale Earnhardt Inc. cars have won six of the last eight races at Daytona and Talladega, the tour's two tracks that require engine restrictor plates to reduce horsepower. Forget everything else that has happened over the last two years because that one statistic represents domination as pure and absolute as anything the sport has to offer these days.

And there is a bit of poetic justice in that Dale Earnhardt, whose style and talent personified superspeedway success, left a legacy at Daytona and Talladega that continues not only through his success but through the team that bears his name. Two years after Earnhardt's death in the fourth turn at Daytona, there is no way to separate his superspeedway legacy from the success of his teams at Daytona and Talladega.

Dale Earnhardt Jr. is keenly aware of the legacy he faces and what his four restrictor-plate wins in eight races mean to his place in the sport.

"It's a good feeling because you grow up kind of battling comparisons with your father, anticipating more comparisons with your father," says Earnhardt Jr. "I watched Davey Allison and Kyle Petty, watched those guys as a kid, knowing well that I was going to be under the same circumstances at some point in time—to have to weather the storm, so to speak—when you didn't live up to your expectations that everyone set for you."

His success at Daytona and Talladega makes Earnhardt Jr. feel like he's doing his part to carry on the Earnhardt name. "That's real important to me, that there's an Earnhardt out there to cheer for, and

doing good enough to cheer for," he says. "That makes me feel good. I just want to keep on racking up accomplishments so that when it's all done I can sit down and say I was a good race car driver and I made my daddy proud."

Shadow of the Intimidator

Dale Earnhardt's success in restrictor-plate races indeed casts a long shadow. He won the 1998 Daytona 500, won twice in the summer race, and won 12 Daytona 500 Twin 125 qualifying races, including 10 straight between 1990 and 1999. He was equally adept at Talladega, winning 10 races at the tour's fastest track.

"Dale Earnhardt put his signature, his stamp, on this sport," says DEI driver Michael Waltrip. "It was

Thanks to a stellar record in restrictor-plate races, Dale Earnhardt Inc., under Teresa Earnhardt's guidance, is a Winston Cup powerhouse with drivers Dale Earnhardt Jr., Steve Park, and Michael Waltrip. *Harold Hinson*

his prowess at Daytona and Talladega, his ability to win plate races. He was the best at it."

DEI cars have twice put Waltrip in victory lane at Daytona (in the 2001 Daytona 500 and in the July race last season), giving the popular driver his only point wins in NASCAR's top series. Waltrip also won a Twin 125 qualifying race last season.

Earnhardt Jr., meanwhile, has prevailed in the last three races at Talladega, and he won the July race at Daytona in 2001.

During their superspeedway domination over the past two seasons, Waltrip and Earnhardt Jr. have finished first and second three times. Junior was second in Waltrip's Daytona 500 win, and Waltrip was second during Earnhardt's win in July 2001 at Daytona and in last season's spring race at Talladega. Steve Park, the third DEI driver, has yet to regain full winning form from injuries he suffered at Darlington in late 2001.

The superspeedway success of Waltrip and Earnhardt Jr. has helped define the past two NASCAR seasons. One of the sport's most endearing and lasting images is Earnhardt Jr.'s win at Daytona in July 2001, just five months after his father's death at the track. The celebration triggered by the victory, when Earnhardt Jr. and Waltrip embraced and celebrated on the track's infield grass, was a triumphant moment for the sport and for DEI. The celebration also foreshadowed DEI's dominant run, as Waltrip and Earnhardt Jr. have won four of the five restrictor-plate races since then.

The Hardware

Other teams have sought the formula to DEI's success with trips to the wind tunnel and extra effort in the engine room.

Greg Zipadelli, crew chief for defending Winston Cup champion Tony Stewart, says that Joe Gibbs Racing, which fields the cars of Stewart and Bobby Labonte, is putting more time and effort into its restrictor-plate program this year. Zipadelli calls DEI "definitely the class of the field" in restrictor-plate racing.

"They've raised the bar as far as restrictor-plate racing, and they're making it a lot harder to catch up to them," says Zipadelli. "They've just paid attention to details a lot more than we have, or more than the other teams have."

"Their organization is obviously on to something because two out of their three cars really run well at the restrictor-plate races," says Bill Wilburn, crew chief for Rusty Wallace. "Michael Waltrip has always been a good speedway driver. That's always been one of the areas, at Daytona and Talladega, where he shines and has been competitive, no matter whose car he drove. So you put those two guys there, with that information in mind, behind a situation with good cars, good engines, and a good thought process behind their program—then, hey, it just breeds success."

In the decade or so since aerodynamics became so vital to NASCAR success, the debate has

The cars of Earnhardt Jr. (8), Park (1), and Waltrip (15) run together at Talladega.

Sam Sharpe

centered on this question: Is aerodynamics or engine performance the key to superspeedway success? The sport used to be populated by engine builders known for their ability to make more horsepower than the competition, and their drivers often found their way to victory lane. Men like Waddell Wilson, Ernie Elliott, and Maurice Petty could power guys like Buddy Baker, Bill Elliott, and Richard Petty to wins at Daytona and Talladega back when Winston Cup cars still looked like passenger cars.

Today, the road to victory lane is paved with an array of components: calculations by engineers, wind tunnel time, research and development in the engine room, constant tweaking of body shapes, and so forth.

"It's like a puzzle—it's no good without all the ingredients," says Buddy Baker, whose 1980 win still stands as the fastest Daytona 500 ever. "If you've got pieces missing, you'll never get it solved. If the motor does not run, then a great body does not mean a great deal. And if the driver is not going to push the button—if you don't take that extra little 10 percent that you have to put into your driving—you're not going to win Talladega and Daytona."

This may be the year for the competition to make up ground on the DEI cars, however. Chevrolet has introduced a new Monte Carlo for the 2003 season, making obsolete much of the body configurations teams have developed.

"It's all kind of up in the air right now as far as how our new bodies are going to work out for us [and] whether we've done our homework in the off-season," says Earnhardt Jr. "It's like almost starting from scratch again. I expect that we'll go and be competitive. I doubt we'll be as strong as we have been there in the past, but I think we'll be a top 10 car, and over the year we'll figure out what it takes to get that car back to where it has been in the past."

"We'll see if the tide changes, but I don't really look for it to change much on either one of their parts," says Wilburn. "Like I said, they're good drivers and they have a good feel for the cars. With restrictor-plate engines and the rules we have to race under, the way you get your race car and the way you're able to handle your car in traffic—basically that feel you have to have for your car to go fast under those restrictions—that's all a big part of it, and I believe those guys have a little better handle on it than anybody else."

Staying Up Front

Another key to DEI's success may be its ability to tweak and tune its engines and bodies, so while a new body style may mean some of the hardware has changed, the engines, the baseline of knowledge, and DEI's willingness to fine-tune its equipment, all remain in place.

"I have to give a tremendous amount of credit to [team manager] Steve Hmiel, [engine builder] Richie Gilmore, and [crew chief] Slugger Labbe," Waltrip said after his win at Daytona last summer. "I had the fastest car and it's because of their effort and DEI's

ability to explore every avenue that is available to us today in order to succeed. We go to the proving grounds in Arizona and we go to the wind tunnel. We go to the shaker machines and shake our cars up and down and we just have all the tools. [In] restrictor-plate racing the car is almost an engineering masterpiece. It's just a feat to get a car that will go fast."

Earnhardt Jr. also credits Gilmore with having a good restrictor-plate engine, one that has a good combination "as far as the cam and where the torque range is in the motor. It just seems to help the car pull up and draft well and be able to make passes."

"The bodies on the cars, they continue to mess with those," he continues. "Even once we're done testing in Daytona throughout the winter and we race our first car at the Daytona 500, they'll come back and cut the sides off of it and try to get it better. When we say it's the same car we race here and the same car we race there, that doesn't mean they haven't moved the nose or moved the tailpiece or worked on the spoiler or changed something to try and get a little better. They send them to the wind tunnel throughout the year to try to improve or try to learn something. I mean, it never ends.

"It used to be you would race a car at Daytona and just put it over in the corner. If you ran good, you would leave it alone and put it in the corner and wait for Talladega to come. But it's not like that anymore."

DEI drivers can also thank Teresa Earnhardt for their continued success. She knew how important Daytona and Talladega were to her late husband and has made sure the team has the resources to stay out front.

"As a driver, Dale did incredible things in restrictor-plate racing," Teresa says. "When we were establishing our goals for our Winston Cup teams years ago, we decided that one of the things we wanted to do as owners was to consistently be a threat on the superspeedways. Restrictor-plate races are among the highest profile events that there are in the sport, so we wanted to be recognized as a leader in that arena.

"Dale personally worked to see that we are among the best. We met the goal we established and invested a great deal of time and resources to see that we stay that way. It was important to Dale and to all of us here at DEI. We take restrictor-plate racing personally."

To help stay among the best, DEI has an alliance with the Richard Childress and Andy Petree teams. The three teams formed RAD (an acronym for Richard, Andy, Dale) Engineering a few seasons ago in order to share wind tunnel and other aerodynamic information. Factor in Petree's win at Talladega in the spring of 2001, with driver Bobby Hamilton, and RAD Engineering has won seven of the last eight restrictor-plate races.

The Earnhardt Factor

During his heyday in the 1970s and 1980s, Buddy Baker had the heaviest foot in the NASCAR garage. Baker, who still works as a test driver for Penske Racing South, knew one speed at Daytona and

Earnhardt Jr. is recognized as a leader in restrictor-plate racing. *Jesse Miles Jr.*

Earnhardt Jr. won at Daytona five months after his father's death. *Harold Hinson*

The July victory at Daytona was a triumphant moment for DEI. *CIA Stock Photography*

Talladega—flat out—but he respects Dale Earnhardt as the man who knew his way around those tracks better than any other.

"At one time," says Baker, "I felt I had a pretty good advantage over most of the guys I was racing against, but he [Earnhardt] epitomized Daytona and Talladega as far as being the man to beat. I dare say, and this is certainly not a reflection against any race team or anything else, but there was a time when you could have put Dale Earnhardt in any of the top five cars and he would have won."

Earnhardt's ability on superspeedways was never more evident than in his last win, in the fall race at Talladega in 2000. "That right there is a perfect example of a guy knowing what he's going to do before you even have a clue what you're going to do," says Wilburn. "I don't believe that they've got a superior car that can run from 20th to first in 10 or 15 laps, or whatever it was. I don't believe anybody has a car like that. In all situations, you've got to be three steps ahead of where you're at right now and anticipate the next guy's moves. It's just a guy capable of making moves, knowing where he's going to be before you're even able to think about where you're going to be. He's already there, and he's just gone. He was always that kind of driver and it didn't change when he got on a speedway."

Wilburn sees the same traits in the next generation. "Dale Earnhardt is gone from us now," he says, "but I think there is one individual named Dale Jr. who might have learned a thing or two and probably had some conversations with his father and picked up a tip or two."

Nonetheless, his father's talent took some time to manifest itself in Earnhardt Jr. His first trip to Daytona, a Busch Series race in 1998, included a broken driveshaft on a pit stop (driver error) and a wild flip on the backstretch (wrong place at the wrong time). There was a pronounced learning curve.

"When you first come in as a rookie, it's really hard to know when to go, when to make a run, when to attempt a pass, and when you need to stay in the draft," says Earnhardt Jr. "It was really hard for me when I first started running at Daytona and Talladega to know when to do that, and when not to, and what was a smart move. . . . So it took me awhile, took me a couple of races, a couple of years. Like in the Busch Series, I crashed out of pretty much every one of the plate races I ran. That was just because I didn't know when to be aggressive and when not to be aggressive and just kept getting myself in the wrong situations.

"Then when you come into the [Winston] Cup series, you've got to know when to be in the low line and you've got to know when to be in the high line.

You've got to know when changing lines is going to improve your position. It's really tough and it's hard to figure that out. I used to race as hard as I could and never get anywhere, almost lose three or four spots. And my dad could whip right up through there, no problem. I would be like, 'Man, how come I keep getting in the wrong line and he seems to keep getting in the right line?' And you just kind of figure that out.

"There's no way to really tell you, 'All right, this is how you get to the front.' You just have to be sitting there in the car when the time comes to know, 'All right, this line is getting ready to move forward three or four lanes. I'm getting in it.' You hop in it and pick up three or four spots and get back to the bottom line and make a few moves there. And you do it without really being aggressive. You hope that when you're done, you're up front and everybody wonders how you got there."

As the 2003 season gets underway, DEI has the competition wondering that very thing: how the team gets to victory lane so often at Talladega and Daytona.

"I know when it comes time to race you only have to win a couple of races in a row and all of a sudden you've placed yourself as a favorite," says Wilburn. "Well, when you've won six out of the last eight, it doesn't take much calculating to figure, hey, we've definitely got to deal with these guys before the day is over."

Earnhardt Jr. and DEI stood tall at Talladega in 2002, sweeping both races. *Harold Hinson*

Daytona Dreams

Of Dale Earnhardt Jr.'s seven wins in three seasons of Winston Cup racing, only one, in July 2001, has come at Daytona International Speedway. Still, he says Daytona is his favorite track.

"Being a driver in the Winston Cup Series, there's nothing like going to the Daytona 500," he says. "There's nothing like running the qualifying races, being a part of the Bud Shootout and the entire Speedweeks, the build-up and the hype and just being there for that long a period.

"These other races, you just bolt in, bolt out, and get your 500 miles in and be satisfied or be disappointed. Then the next week is here before you know it. But Speedweeks [are] anticipated throughout the off-season, and it's the best feeling when you get there."

Which would mean more at this stage of his career, a win in the Daytona 500 or a top five finish in points?

"Oh, definitely. I would take the win in the 500 over a top five in points," he says. "A top five in points would be great for the team. We want to win the championship one of these days and you've got to keep getting closer before you do that. But, I don't know, I want to get a Daytona 500 win under my belt before I hang it up."

KEVIN HARVICK

4

Born: December 8, 1975

Hometown: Bakersfield, California

Height: 5-10

Weight: 175 lbs.

Sponsor	**GM Goodwrench Service**
Make	**Chevrolet**
Crew Chief	**Todd Berrier**
Owner	**Richard Childress**

NASCAR Winston Cup Career Statistics

Year	Races	Wins	Top 5s	Top 10s	Poles	Total Points	Final Standing	Winnings
2001	35	2	6	16	0	4,406	9	$4,302,202
2002	35	1	5	8	1	3,501	21	$3,704,605
Totals	70	3	11	24	1	7,907		$8,006,807

Kevin Harvick's No. 29 car got a new look for 2003, with stylized flames added to the side. *Nigel Kinrade*

A RACER'S EDUCATION

BY LARRY WARREN
From *Stock Car Racing*, February 1999

Kevin Harvick Learned About Racing from His Father. Now at Age 23 He's One of the Top Drivers in Two Tough NASCAR Circuits

Kevin Harvick grew up watching his father, Mike, build race cars. *SCR Archives*

Success in racing, as in any profession, requires a good education. There is no better example of this than Kevin Harvick's recent meteoric rise. At age 23, Harvick already has 14 years of racing experience. He has won races and championships in go karts, late models, and NASCAR's Southwest Tour and Winston West series. In 1998 he competed in both the Winston West and Craftsman Truck Series.

Harvick started racing when his father Mike gave him a go kart as a kindergarten graduation present. "I wanted a father-and-son thing we could do together when Kevin got old enough, and go karts were perfect," recalls Mike.

Mike is a Bakersfield, California, firefighter by profession and a racing mechanic by avocation. Firemen have lots of time off, and he found a way to put his to good use by starting a small race car repair business. Eventually he became a force in local racing, serving as crew chief for several front-runners, including Rick Carelli.

The success of the race car fabrication shop allowed Mike and Kevin to pursue go kart racing. "We took off and never looked back," Mike says. They traveled the country from the time Kevin was 8 till he was 16, winning several regional and national go kart championships.

It soon became obvious that Harvick had a natural feel for racing and a maturity beyond his years. Mike knew from experience that Kevin needed to temper his talent with the hard lessons that make a driver into a racer.

"Anyone can win races at their own home track," explains Mike. "The guys who can win at any track—those are the real race drivers. I wanted Kevin to learn this, so in karts we traveled to as many different tracks as possible."

In 1993 Mike acquired a late-model sportsman car as payment for his work as a crew chief. He knew the time had come for 15-year-old Kevin to graduate from go karts to the Winston Racing Series late models at Mesa Marin Raceway.

"It was certainly a different feel," Harvick says of the transition to full-size cars. "It was intimidating at first, climbing into a stock car. The basics were the same as in karts, but you were throwing a big, heavy car around and it took some getting used to."

As in the karts, Mike taught his son all the lessons a young driver should learn about stock car racing. Even the tough ones. "He consistently put setups in the car that felt good to me," Harvick remembers. "But sometimes he put me in situations so I would know what it felt like to drive a car that wasn't right."

Harvick ran seven races that first year and mostly crashed. "After sitting around and thinking about it over the winter, he learned from experience," recalls Mike ruefully. The next year Harvick won 7 of the 15 races he ran at Mesa Marin and the 1995 late-model championship.

He won four of the six races he ran in 1996. Mike then sold the late model and built a Featherlite Southwest Tour car. "There was a lot of good competitive racing in the tour and that was what Kevin needed," Mike says. Harvick won the rookie of the year title, along with the Tucson round of the tour.

"We didn't have much money and never tested," Harvick says. "All we really had was know-how. The fact that we didn't have a lot of money was actually a plus, because it taught me how to take care of equipment and get in as many laps as possible. The experience I got running at the different tracks was very useful later on."

By the time the 1996 season rolled around, the Harvick racing team was out of money. "Then right at the end of the year, Wayne Spears called me to drive his Winston West car," Harvick says. "I had never driven a Winston West car."

Spears, a longtime Winston West team owner, had seen Harvick race at Mesa Marin and was impressed. Harvick qualified fourth and finished tenth in his first race. "The biggest problem I had in adapting to these cars was that I had never been on a [super] speedway, or raced on radial tires," he says. "And I sure had never dealt with that much horsepower."

Spears liked what he saw, and in 1997 he ran Harvick in half the Craftsman truck schedule and three Winston West races. In 1998 Harvick ran the full schedules in both Winston West and Craftsman series. This was his opportunity to put the finishing touches on his racing education.

He passed this final exam with flying colors, dominating Winston West and competing successfully against much more experienced drivers in the Craftsman series. He finished out the season with the championship in Winston West. He won five races, more than anyone else in the series, and five poles, also more than any other driver. His truck racing year included some very strong runs and 17th place in points.

Harvick's years of training and experience kept rookie mistakes to a minimum and allowed his natural ability to shine. "Nazareth is one of the trickiest tracks on the circuit, and Harvick had it down after only three laps with no practice," Spears says. Harvick learned the track with no sleep. He had flown all night on a red-eye from California, where he had run a Winston West race.

Kevin Harvick's racing future is bright. After graduating from high school and attending college for a year and a half, he decided that racing was what he wanted to do. "I want to race Winston Cup someday," he says. "Wayne and Connie Spears have given me the opportunity to race in first-class equipment. There's not much more a 23-year-old kid could ask for."

The young racer is quick to give his father credit for his racing education. "My father's experience got me where I am right now," he says. "The most important thing he taught me was communication. He never pushed me to race. He only pushed me to do my best."

Kevin was nearly five years old when this photo was taken. *SCR Archives*

Kevin's kindergarten graduation present was a go kart. *SCR Archives*

RACING GIFTS

From *Stock Car Racing*, July 1999

Harvick was 12th in Craftsman Truck Series points in 1999, racing the For F-150 Porter Cable truck. *SCR Archives*

Kevin Harvick feels that he stacked the deck in his favor when he signed on with the No. 98 Porter-Cable Power Tools Ford F-150 Liberty Racing team. Competing full time on two NASCAR touring series last year, this young 23-year-old performed the astonishing feat of winning the Winston West championship and did a stellar job in his Craftsman truck, finishing 17th in points, qualifying second at Louisville, and placing fourth at Texas.

He also won the 1998 Coors 200 Southwest Tour Series race at Mesa Marin in California. For those outstanding achievements, the Motorsports Press Association named him driver of the year.

He's competed in each of the first four seasons in the Craftsman Truck Series, with 45 career starts under his belt. Only three races into this season, and he has already posted two top 10 qualifying efforts. "With Signature Racing Engines, I feel we have one of the top five engine programs," says Harvick.

"Being a brand-new team for me, we'll have our ups and downs at first, but I think we're going to win a couple races this year, if not more. Whatever happens, we'll be a tall contender every week."

He considers this new team an early Christmas present. "At our banquet last year in San Francisco, Ron Hornaday struck up a conversation with Tim Stephens, Liberty Racing's team manager. That following Monday, I got a phone call from Tim. At the end of that week, I was in Ohio."

Another gift was his new crew chief, Roland Wlodyka, who, at 60, has decades of NASCAR Winston Cup knowledge under his belt.

"Roland's a walking pile of information for me," says Harvick. "We get along so well that it's almost scary. He knows that he needs to put the reins on me sometimes, but I'm learning a lot from him."

With his eye on a future Busch or Winston Cup ride, Harvick states that the new television package for the Craftsman Series will let the fans get to better know the drivers. "It helps people like me who are actually good race drivers make a name for themselves."

THE SKY'S THE LIMIT

BY JERRY F. BOONE
From *Stock Car Racing*, August 2001

Three days after his friend and mentor died at Daytona, 25-year-old Kevin Harvick arrived for work in a job he really didn't want.

"I went into the trailer, and at first I couldn't bring myself to put my gear in his locker," Harvick says. "It just didn't seem right. I had to fight with myself to do it."

The racing world was still in shock from Dale Earnhardt's death in the final lap of the Daytona 500 when Harvick was named to replace him at Richard Childress Racing.

"Richard called and I told him I would do whatever the team needed me to do," he says.

Immediately Harvick went from being an emerging talent in the Busch Series to among the most recognizable faces in NASCAR.

It is the face of a clean-cut kid who grew up knowing he wanted to race. He could be a poster boy for everything good about motorsports. Handsome. Articulate. Successful. And still humble.

Fans crowd around the rear of both his Winston Cup and Busch Series transporters, pleading for an autograph or a quick picture.

"It can be pretty overwhelming," Harvick says.

The rush was especially strong at California Speedway during his first "homecoming" to southern California in the spring. "There's just so many family and friends here," he says. "There's just so little time for everything."

Beginnings

For Harvick, southern California is where it all began.

His first memory of a race car was the view from behind bars in his dad's garage.

"We didn't have much money," Harvick says. "My folks set up a playpen in my father's race shop."

"We spent a lot of time together," says his father, Mike Harvick, who works as a firefighter and runs Mike's Motorsports in Bakersfield. "When he was real small, most of that was babysitting."

"I was either in the playpen or putting parts on the cars where they probably didn't belong," Kevin says.

So while other kids were learning their ABCs from *Sesame Street*, young Kevin Harvick was being schooled in carb jetting and suspension settings.

For his kindergarten graduation, his dad gave him a go kart. Harvick spent the next 10 years racing go karts on local road courses.

"I don't think there's a better way to learn," Harvick says. "You learn car control, weight transfer, how to drive in traffic, how to make the best use of the power you have."

Harvick followed his dad into stock car racing and then moved into the car made famous by Dale Earnhardt. *Doug Miller*

In 1994, Harvick raced at Mesa Marin, California, and entered a few Featherlite races. *SCR Archives*

Kevin Harvick, shown here in 1984 with his sister, Amber, says go karting taught him much about racing. *SCR Archives*

Harvick says he still feels Dale Earnhardt's presence every time he buckles himself into the race car. *Harold Hinson*

The karting experience headed him toward an interest in open-wheel cars that go both left and right.

"I grew up watching the Indy 500 and dreaming of someday racing in it," he says. "But Dad was into stock cars, so that's what he built for me when it was time to move up. I guess now that isn't such a bad thing."

Stock Cars

"It was the stock car shop that paid for his racing," Mike says. "We had to work to race. We built stock cars, so that's what we raced."

The move from a tiny go kart to a fully prepared NASCAR late model as soon as he turned 16 was a huge leap. Actually, he may have been driving a late model slightly before that.

"We might have snuck him [in] a little early," Mike says. Kevin made his late-model debut at Mesa Marin Speedway in Bakersfield. Marion Collins, who runs the track and is a longtime friend of the Harvick family, says he expected to see the young Harvick racing there one day.

"He was always hanging around the track," Collins says. "I think I've known him since he was five or six."

Collins calls Harvick his "rent-a-kid" because he used to borrow the youngster to go to Disney movies when his own youngsters got too old to enjoy the shows.

"He started racing here when he was still in school," says Collins. "Mike and Kevin worked together on the cars. His dad was with him right up until Kevin started to get offers of rides. Mike's a fantastic chassis man."

"I don't remember my first drive in the late model," Harvick says, "but I'm pretty sure I crashed it. If I didn't, it was one of the few races that first year I didn't tear it up."

"There was a time when Kevin was just beginning that I wondered if either one of us [was] going to survive the first season. He tore up stuff every night," says Mike. "When he was 15, he didn't do anything but wreck. One time he wrecked and caught on fire. I think that one got his attention."

"I guess it was just that my dad kept telling me what not to do . . . then I'd turn around and do it. And then I'd wreck the car," Harvick jokes.

Opportunities

Eventually, Harvick figured out that you had to finish to win, and he began doing that regularly. He became a popular young standout at Mesa Marin, winning a championship there in his second year. He ran some races in NASCAR's Featherlite Southwest Series, a regional touring division for late models, and he was good enough to get an offer for a one-time ride in the Craftsman Truck Series.

Soon, Harvick's talent exceeded the family budget.

"We didn't have the money to afford to take him where he wanted to go," Mike says. "The only way he was going to make a career of this was to move on to a professional team. I understood that."

Harvick was running late models at Mesa Marin when he was spotted by an engine builder for Spears Racing.

"We were going to run a second truck and put him in it. I don't remember how he did, but I remember he finished in the top 10 in the next race," says Spears Racing's Al Hoffman. "We decided that we liked him. We knew he had a lot of talent and he sure could drive."

"Once he got comfortable in a vehicle, he was a serious contender," Hoffman says. "Having Kevin around made everyone want to work for him."

Learning Curve

Ron Hornaday Jr. has raced against Harvick in the Featherlite Southwest Series, Craftsman Truck Series, Busch Series, and now in the Winston Cup Series.

"He hasn't changed a bit," Hornaday says. "He always drove hard and went for the win. He still does."

Hoffman says that Harvick has changed in the level of experience and his ability to tell a crew what he needs.

"There were times he just couldn't be specific enough for us to help him with the truck," he says. "It is something that just takes time to learn."

Harvick was just a bit better than a midpack driver in the Craftsman Truck Series. He failed to either win or take a pole in 69 starts. He recorded nine top five finishes and nine more in the top 10.

"He always ran flat out in the trucks," says Stacy Compton, also a veteran of the truck series who races against Harvick in Winston Cup. "He was pretty wild sometimes . . . but I guess we all were in the truck series.

"He's really changed since then. Now he knows you have to finish to win."

"I think Kevin was better than his equipment," adds Greg Biffle, who shared the track with Harvick in the truck series and is battling with him this season in the Busch Series. "I think it was a case that he didn't have enough experience and his team didn't have the same resources as some of the others."

Harvick also ended up being spread thin.

"He really wanted to drive cars," remembers Hoffman. So to keep the young driver in their truck, Spears Manufacturing added a car for the Winston West Series. Harvick ran 52 races in 1998, at times running a Winston West race on Friday night and taking the red-eye flight across

Despite the pressure of taking over for Dale Earnhardt, the rookie Harvick won early in the 2001 season at Atlanta. *Harold Hinson*

the country to compete in the Craftsman Truck Series at an eastern track like Bristol.

"Kevin learned patience," Hoffman says, "and he learned to take it easy on the equipment. He ran the entire Winston West Series on one car."

Not only did he run it, he took the championship with five wins in 14 starts. Eleven of his finishes were in the top 10.

Enter Richard Childress

It was that kind of performance that attracted attention from Richard Childress in 1999.

"We were at Martinsville when Richard Childress asked me about racing for him," Harvick says. "I was in the Porter Cable truck and still wasn't doing really well. The trucks were a great opportunity, but I never was on a team that had the same resources the big ones had.

"He asked me if I'd be interested in doing the Busch Series for him. I guess he figured out that I could drive better than the results showed."

In 31 Busch Series starts, Harvick collected three wins, two poles, and finished third in the

Kevin Harvick Career Highlights

1980
Received his first race car, a road course go kart. In the next 10 years, he would win seven national championships and two Grand National Go Kart championships.

1992
Rookie in the NASCAR late-model division at Mesa Marin Raceway, Bakersfield, California.

1993
NASCAR late-model champion at Mesa Marin. Ran some NASCAR Featherlite Southwest Series races.

1994
Raced at Mesa Marin and entered a few Featherlite races.

1995
Rookie of the year in Featherlite Southwest Series. Won one race at Tucson Raceway Park and finished 11th in points.

1997
Split his time between racing and attending Bakersfield Junior College. Began racing for Spears Manufacturing in the NASCAR Craftsman Truck Series.

1998
Won the NASCAR Winston West championship while also racing for Spears in the Craftsman Truck Series. Named the Motorsports Press Association's Closed Wheel Driver of the Year.

1999
Finished 12th in Craftsman Truck Series points racing in the Porter Cable truck. Ran two ARCA races, finishing second at Charlotte and third at Talladega.

2000
Rookie of the year in the NASCAR Busch Series, finishing third in series points with wins at St. Louis, Bristol, and Memphis. Won Bud Pole Award at Dover and Bristol. Tied two series records for rookies: most wins and highest finishing position (third).

2001
Named to replace the late Dale Earnhardt at Richard Childress Racing. Won his third race in the renumbered 29 car at Atlanta Motor Speedway. Continued to drive the ACDelco Chevrolet full time in the NASCAR Busch Series.

points to become the 2000 rookie of the year. He finished 16 races—that's 50 percent—in the top 10.

"Along the way he developed the brains to go along with his guts," says Harvick's dad.

He also ended up doing a lot of testing for Earnhardt.

"It wasn't supposed to be part of the job at first," Harvick says, but it worked out well for the team.

Harvick could work with the Earnhardt crew while "The Intimidator" took care of his business interests, mentoring his son and developing his own DEI team. "The whole plan was that when Dale retired, he would have someone ready to step in," Harvick says. So when Childress picked him to fill in for Earnhardt, it made sense. He had already turned thousands of laps in Earnhardt's Monte Carlo.

"The team knew me and we had worked a lot together," he says. "They had a pretty good idea of what I need in the car. I think my driving style and Dale's was pretty close. That's why I could work with the team on his car.

"It made the transition a lot easier."

Earnhardt's Shadow

Still, it was difficult to try to replace a man who is irreplaceable. Some fans wondered if this youngster with the Eagle Scout poster boy looks could do the job.

He answered them three races later when he won at Atlanta, holding off a charging Jeff Gordon for the win. Harvick did a "Polish victory lap" in honor of his friend and mentor, and to compose himself before facing the crowds and cameras.

He says Earnhardt's death meant the loss of a mentor to him.

"But there's a lot of guys on the team who help," he says. "Richard Childress has probably had the most impact. He's taught me how to drive for points. I used to drive for laps. Sometimes I forget or get excited and I still do. But that doesn't get you a lot of wins.

"My dad used to tell me that, but I never paid any attention to him."

Harvick wants to be the top rookie in Winston Cup and challenge for the championship in the Busch Series. He says there's still a lot of expectations—some of them higher than they should be—on him and the team.

"There's a lot of people who still want to believe Dale's still in the car. They expect the same results. I think that will go away with time. I'm still a rookie in Winston Cup," he says. "The team has a lot of experience, so they expect more from us than if we were all beginning this together.

"I think that a lot of fans outside maybe expect too much. I think the expectation inside the team is realistic."

The car's colors are different. The number has been changed. But inside, it is still Dale's car. Harvick says he still feels Earnhardt's presence in it every time he buckles in for a race.

"It will always be Dale's car," Harvick says. "This will always be the team that he and Richard Childress built over all those years.

"And that's not a bad thing."

HARVICK ON HIS FIRST SEASON

BY JASON MITCHELL
From *Stock Car Racing*, March 2002

To some he's one of the best young talents to ever enter the big leagues of stock car racing. To others, he's an overly aggressive wise guy trying to achieve too much too soon. Kevin Harvick's accomplishments can't be ignored, nor can the fender-banging driving style that occasionally got him into hot water last season. Harvick sat down with *Stock Car Racing* to reflect on the lessons learned from his first year of Winston Cup racing, his Busch Series championship, and the new season that lies ahead.

How did you pull off what you did in both the NASCAR Winston Cup Series and the Busch Series in 2001?

Most of what we accomplished last year came from the strength of Richard Childress Racing, which is cut from a pretty strong mold as a whole. They were able to fly me here and there last year to race in both divisions without having to depend on anybody else. There are a lot of good people involved in a lot of areas within this organization that kept everything flowing in the right direction.

Were there times when you got tired of being pulled in so many directions?

There were a lot of times when I wondered what in the heck I was trying to do. A good example of that is after the Busch Series race in St. Louis where I laid on the plane getting an IV put in my arm. Then again, I had to remember that odd circumstances required me and everybody else on the team to make it work. That's what kept us going, along with all the critics who said there was no way I could do both.

How do you think you handled everything last year?

For the most part, I wasn't as close to Dale Earnhardt as a lot of the people were who'd been around this team for a while. Even with that, those same people were behind me from the get-go and they made that very clear. But when the emotions were running low, like when we went to Rockingham and Atlanta, there was always somebody around to help pick things up. For the most part, I think the fact that I wasn't that close to Dale probably helped some, but I still had to remember the circumstances that put me where I am. Everybody really had to come together as one.

You did ultimately complete your dream of winning a Busch Series championship. What does that mean to you?

Winning the Busch Series championship meant a great deal to me. Not only that, but we also won

Harvick's style has drawn mixed reactions from his competitors. *Nigel Kinrade*

rookie of the year and finished in the top 10 in Winston Cup points. That's something that nobody had ever done before, and I feel like that says a lot about the strength of this organization. It's something that will probably never be done again, and since it had never been done before, that does mean a great deal to me personally. Nobody thought we could do it.

What do you feel was your greatest accomplishment in 2001?

To be honest, just making it through the season in both divisions. We made all the Winston Cup races and we've run very consistently in both Busch and Cup. We set out to run 70 races and we ran 70 races. It's almost mind-boggling when you sit back and look at all we did last year. It's overwhelming when you think about it.

Harvick had little downtime in 2001 as he competed full time in both Winston Cup and Busch. *Sam Sharpe*

Harvick was strong from the day the team first unloaded his No. 29 car at Rockingham in February. *Nigel Kinrade*

"If you're going to dish it out, you have to be willing to take it too. Some of the guys like to complain about people driving rough. I just give it back to them on the track. I can dish it out, but I can take it too."

—Kevin Harvick

On top of all the racing last year, you actually found the time to get married before the race at Las Vegas. How much help has DeLana been as far as dealing with everything?

Aside from Richard Childress, DeLana has probably been the strongest thing holding me together through all I went through last year. When something's going bad, she can always get me in a good mood or set me straight on how I need to be thinking. She's definitely been one of the strongest two assets to me.

What did you do over the winter to get away from racing before going to Daytona for testing?

Toward the end of last year everybody asked where I was going in the off-season. I stayed at home. We stayed on the road so much last year, we just wanted to spend some time to learn things like our address and zip code. We just relaxed.

But didn't you still owe DeLana a honeymoon?

Yeah, but she didn't get it. Seriously, she didn't want it either because staying at home over the winter was something she really wanted to do too. DeLana was as content to stay at home as I was because she was on every plane ride and went to every race with me last year. It's been as hard on her as it has on me.

Outside of racing, what's a perfect day in the life of Kevin Harvick?

Really, just spending time and relaxing. I like playing with the dogs and my radio-controlled cars. I also have an arcade downstairs at home, so I like messing with that, too. If I've got time off, I just like to kick back and not do a lot.

How do you explain your driving style?

It's aggressive and always has been. I was always pushed to figure out why I wasn't winning even when I finished second. Doing what you have to do to win is how I was taught to race. That's how my father taught me to race, with a "do what you have to do to win" attitude because nothing else matters.

Sometimes your driving style ruffled the feathers of your fellow drivers. What's your take on that?

That's OK with me. If you're going to dish it out, you have to be willing to take it too. Some of the guys like to complain about people driving rough. I just give it back to them on the track. I can dish it out, but I can take it too. Those guys complaining about me aren't going to change me, so I'm going to continue doing what I have to do to win races.

After winning the Busch Series title, you made the comment that you realized you'd made some mistakes. What did you mean by that? Were you maybe at times too aggressive?

I don't think most of my mistakes were made on the track. Most of my mistakes were made after the races when my emotions were running high. I guess I need to learn to compose myself a little bit quicker. I think over the course of last year, I learned to become a lot better at that. Just knowing when to say what at the right time and when not to say something at the wrong time is probably the biggest thing I learned last year. But as far as on the track, I don't feel like I need to change too much.

Following the fall Winston Cup race at Martinsville, a fellow driver said you were trying to fill Dale Earnhardt's shoes and driving over your head. How do you take that?

All of us would give back everything we did last year if we could have Dale Earnhardt with us, but we can't do that. I didn't ask to be put in this position, but I think a lot of people don't realize that I have to

Harvick says he knew the team could win a race during the 2001 season, but admits he was surprised the first victory came so soon at Atlanta. *Nigel Kinrade*

be in this spot in order to keep going. Racing is how we as a team eat and pay our bills. This is our way of life and we have to somehow keep it going. I think comments like those are almost made out of resentment because I'm only 26 years old and doing good. They're looking for the easiest way to excuse themselves of getting beat by a 26-year-old. To me, those were some cheap comments.

Do you fear being labeled as an overaggressive driver by your peers?

That doesn't bother me in the least.

What's the biggest thing you learned last year?

Richard told me that Winston Cup racing was going to be different, and he didn't quite know how to explain it. He told me I was just going to have to experience it and he was exactly right. It's something that's so big, no matter what you do is huge. The biggest thing I learned was how to deal with all that and being under the microscope. I feel like the lessons I learned last season are going to take me long into my career.

What was the biggest surprise of last season?

It had to be winning at Atlanta. We were just going to the racetracks trying to make it through the weekends at that point because it was so soon after what happened in Daytona. We unloaded off the trailer and were good all weekend. We ended up winning the race very unexpectedly. We thought we would be capable of winning a race later in the year, but not that soon. We were all kind of shocked. It was way above us. You couldn't have written a book any better. We had some ugly circumstances to start the year off, but then to beat Jeff Gordon to the checkered flag was just incredible.

What area do you think you need to improve upon most heading into your second season of Winston Cup?

If I've got a car that's running 10th, that's where I need to finish and not wreck and finish 30th. We need to take the same philosophy we used last year in the Busch Series and turn those bad days into days that aren't that bad. We just need to build on our consistency.

Looking ahead to next year, you're going to be working with a couple of new teammates at RCR. What are your thoughts on the addition of Jeff Green and Robby Gordon?

The addition of those two guys is really going to help this team. Robby's going to have a little bit of a learning curve, but Jeff is probably going to be the biggest asset to the situation. All three of us really want to win and that's going to be good for everybody involved now that we're under the same ownership.

What are your thoughts as you prepare for your first start in the Daytona 500?

It's the biggest stock car race there is, so I can't wait to go there and get the year started off right. Maybe I can win my first Daytona 500. That is the

biggest race in our sport, so winning it would really mean the world to me.

What kind of goals have you set for yourself and the No. 29 team?

The biggest thing we want to do is contend for the championship, and I know that's setting some pretty lofty goals. I really think we can finish somewhere in the top five. Plus I'd like to be in contention to win a few more races.

What is one thing that nobody knows about Kevin Harvick that you think would surprise your fans?

I like to sing to myself for some reason. I'm a car-singer, the guy you see going down the road singing a song that he really doesn't know the words to. I know my wife would tell you that story.

You've obviously got a tremendous amount of racing experience under your belt. But looking back on it all, what is the dumbest thing you've ever done in a race car, something you did and thought, "I can't believe I just did that?"

I think the stupidest thing I ever did was when I was racing my go kart at Riverside in 1991 at the Grand Nationals. I was 15 years old and racing against some of the best drivers there were because they'd been racing for years. I started around seventh, and I was always notorious for going from the back to the front on the first lap. So I slammed that go kart into the grass and slipped back up the track and made it four-wide. I had everybody in the race pissed off at me, but I thought it was pretty cool at the time. Those guys weren't very happy with me.

Harvick ran out front enough in 2001 that he's set high goals for himself in 2002, including a top-five finish in points. *Harold Hinson*

Some competitors say Harvick uses his bumper far too often, but Harvick doesn't apologize for being aggressive. *Sam Sharpe*

TOUGH GUYS, TOUGH TIMES

BY LARRY COTHREN
From *Stock Car Racing*, September 2002

While His Drivers Sometimes Self-Destruct,

Richard Childress Works to Rev Up

His Three-Car Team

Harvick has often been at the center of a tumultuous 2002 season for Richard Childress Racing. *Doug Miller*

As the sound of cars roaring around the track is muffled by the walls of the hauler for his No. 29 Goodwrench Chevrolet, Richard Childress talks about his three-car team's struggles this season, paying equal attention to questions coming his way and practice speeds being posted on a monitor inside the hauler.

"I've been here," Childress says of the sport that has consumed more than 30 years of his life. "We've had bad years. We had bad years before with [Mike] Skinner. We've had bad years with Dale [Earnhardt]. We had four or five bad years and everybody had written Dale off in '97. We came back in '98 and really ran good, won races.

"Sometimes you don't understand—this is a really humbling sport. You don't understand sometimes why you're running good and why you're winning races and why everything is really working. Then all of a sudden it can go the other way just as quick. You can't understand why the caution flag comes out or why it seems you get hung up in all these crashes and stuff. That's part of the business. It's a tough business to be in."

Tough is being redefined at RCR this season, as drivers Jeff Green, Robby Gordon, and Kevin Harvick have spent much of the season trying to claw their way up the points ladder. By the time the schedule was one-third complete, Green was 23rd in points, tops among the group, besting Gordon's 29th and Harvick's 33rd. All were winless.

It's not just the lack of wins and the poor points showing that have hounded RCR. Rumors have circulated about other teams attempting to steal Harvick away, and Gordon appears to get no respect on the track. During the running of The Winston, NASCAR's annual all-star event, Kurt Busch spun Gordon out, then, in post-race interviews, admitted to doing it on purpose in order to bring out a caution. And there are the incidents at Bristol and Martinsville involving Harvick, which together led NASCAR to suspend Harvick from the Winston Cup race at Martinsville.

Even without all the wild stuff, this is not going to be a typical year for RCR. Childress expected growing pains from adding a third car to the mix, while also bringing in two new drivers and building a new shop to house all three cars in an integration process intended to mold the teams into one unit.

"We knew it's like anything in any business besides racing: Sometimes you've got to take a step backwards to go two forward, and we think that's hurt us a little," says Childress. "But we do see the daylight hopefully at the end of the tunnel, and it's not the train."

Eye of the Storm

Yet the organization that twice put Harvick in victory lane as a Winston Cup rookie last year, while also guiding him to the Busch Series driving championship, and the organization that finished the 2001 season by giving Gordon his first Cup win was surprisingly weak in the early part of the schedule. It recorded just two top 10s and four top 12s in the first dozen races.

"You've just got to take it and never give up," says Childress. "You just never give up, and you just know that you're better than where you're running and where you're finishing."

In an attempt to improve performance, Childress announced in late May that he would swap the entire crews of the Harvick and Gordon cars. The decision came during the week after the Coca-Cola 600, an event in which Harvick finished 34th and Gordon 16th. Childress' decision was not totally without precedent at RCR. In 1998, Childress reversed the roles of his crew chiefs, putting Kevin Hamlin with Earnhardt's No. 3 car while placing Larry McReynolds with the No. 31 car of Skinner.

Childress makes no secret of his preference for drivers who race aggressively. It was a style that made a legend of Dale Earnhardt and helped deliver six Winston Cup titles to Childress' Welcome, North

"There's obviously situations where you're going to want to go up and knock the hell out of somebody and know you're not going to be able to do it, and probably don't need to anyway."

—Kevin Harvick

Carolina, shop. Aggressive action isn't limited to the track with RCR's current group of drivers, however.

At the spring Busch Series race at Bristol, Harvick's car hit the wall after getting a nudge from Greg Biffle. Harvick was knocked from the event but waited for Biffle to exit his car at the conclusion of the race. With television cameras in tow, Harvick rushed Biffle, hurdled the rear deck lid of Biffle's car, and grabbed the collar of Biffle's uniform. The two stayed locked up, nose to nose, as Harvick screamed at Biffle. NASCAR responded by fining Harvick $15,000 and placing him on probation until August 28.

The next day at Bristol, Gordon and Dale Earnhardt Jr. tangled after the Winston Cup race. Gordon spun Earnhardt Jr.'s car around on pit road. NASCAR slapped Gordon with a $10,000 fine and, like Harvick, placed him on probation until August 28.

After heading for Texas, the Winston Cup Series rolled into Martinsville. Harvick entered a Craftsman Truck Series race the day before the Winston Cup event. During the truck race, Harvick spun out Coy Gibbs' truck, and NASCAR ordered Harvick off the track. The sanctioning body then suspended Harvick from the next day's race, fined him $35,000, and extended his probation until the end of the calendar year. The one-race suspension was unprecedented in Winston Cup.

The next day Childress chastised NASCAR for the suspension: "NASCAR had to do something in response to Kevin's actions during the truck race yesterday, but I think their response was completely wrong. I have not seen the clip of Kevin's actions during the truck race so I can't comment on what he did. He has had problems in the Busch and truck series and had been on probation for his actions, but the decision to 'park' him during the Winston Cup race is wrong. NASCAR should keep the actions and punishments separate to each series."

Searching for the Right Mix

A contrite Harvick issued a statement two days after the Martinsville race, saying the suspension "definitely got my attention." He also said, "I'm still learning how NASCAR works and what is involved in the decisions they make."

Asked later to elaborate on what he learned from the Martinsville incident, Harvick says the sport has "a lot of politics." He then talks about the far-reaching ramifications of his actions. "The politics are magnified," he says. "The media is magnified. Everything is magnified times 100 compared to what it's like anywhere else. Like I said, I learned a lot in that situation. The biggest thing I learned is how many branches are hanging off our tree, and there's a bunch."

Five weeks after Harvick's suspension, Childress, sitting in the No. 29 hauler, was asked if he could have done more to prevent Harvick's Martinsville blowup. "Not really," he says. "I look at all the things that built up to it. Oh sure, right now I would tell him, 'Hey, you can't go out and do that.' But I don't know the whole story—I wasn't there. As far as being able to comment on it, it just was one of them deals that we all wished hadn't happened, and Kevin wished hadn't happened. All of us do. It wasn't good for any of us.

"I have told him, 'You're going to have to keep driving as hard and, yeah, you may get in a little

Harvick has often been on the losing end in 2002. *Rusty Huband*

"We knew it's like anything in any business besides racing: Sometimes you've got to take a step backwards to go two forward, and we think that's hurt us a little. But we do see the daylight hopefully at the end of the tunnel, and it's not the train."

—Richard Childress

trouble. You've got to stay on it, but you've got to be smart. You've got to be smart in whatever you do. That's the difference—you've got to be smart.'"

When asked if he feels handcuffed by NASCAR, Harvick answers swiftly. "Oh no," he says. "The day that they handcuff me and tell me that I can't race, I'll quit."

While there are parts of his driving style Harvick says he will change, he doesn't plan to remake himself as a driver.

"There's obviously situations where you're going to want to go up and knock the hell out of somebody and know you're not going to be able to do it, and probably don't need to anyway," says Harvick. "It's something that the day that I can't race is the day that I don't want to be here."

Harvick was placed on probation by NASCAR officials because he locked up with Greg Biffle after a Bush Series race at Bristol. *Nigel Kinrade*

Tantrums and Tangles

March 23: Greg Biffle bumps Kevin Harvick's Goodwrench Chevrolet in the Busch Series race at Bristol Motor Speedway, sending Harvick into the wall and out of the race. Harvick waits for Biffle to finish the race, runs toward Biffle's car, hurdles the deck lid, and charges Biffle, grabbing his collar. Standing nose to nose, the two lock arms for nearly a minute as Harvick shouts into Biffle's face. The incident earns Harvick a $15,000 fine and NASCAR probation until August 28.

March 24: After trading bumps with Dale Earnhardt Jr. several times during Bristol's Food City 500, Robby Gordon carries the fray off the track. As the two head down pit road, Gordon bumps Earnhardt Jr.'s car from behind, spinning it around. Later, Gordon is quoted as saying, "I don't know what I did to make him mad but, hey, nobody runs into me." Gordon is fined $10,000 and placed on NASCAR probation until August 28.

April 13: Harvick places the nose of his Craftsman truck under the rear bumper of Coy Gibbs' truck during a race at Martinsville Speedway. Gibbs spins out and NASCAR immediately orders Harvick off the track. Harvick then drives all the way to the NASCAR trailer, parks his truck, and gets out. Harvick is subsequently "parked" by NASCAR for the Winston Cup event the next day. NASCAR later announces a $35,000 fine and a probationary period extending to the end of the calendar year.

ATTITUDE ADJUSTMENT

BY BENNY PHILLIPS
From *Stock Car Racing*, August 2002

Not often, just every once in awhile, there comes along a driver with a holier-than-thou attitude. He probably means well and may be honest, but there is this thing called an attitude adjustment. That is the adult way of saying NASCAR has to take him out behind the woodshed and set his mind straight. And no matter what you think at times, the sport is not going to hell because of a driver, or several drivers. It has been there and done that and handles it well.

Kevin Harvick felt the sting of NASCAR's paddle in April, and by now I would venture to say that he has straightened up considerably or is racing Saturday-night events on some outlaw circuit, chasing the $200 winner's share of the feature purse. Harvick seemingly tried to embarrass NASCAR at Martinsville in the Saturday preliminary race. The sanctioning body parked him after he spun another driver. Harvick parked his racer in NASCAR's front door and went to his motor home where he figured the cushions were more comfortable than in the NASCAR office.

NASCAR got his attention. The sanctioning body fined him $35,000 and would not let him drive in the Winston Cup event on Sunday. The following week at Talladega, he remained unapologetic, saying he did not think he needed to apologize to anyone. He did say he learned a lot about NASCAR's disciplinary style. I bet he did, but it's obvious there are things Harvick does not realize about racing but will learn if he graduates to the next level. If he fails, it is bye-bye—out of sight, out of mind.

Some of you may not understand what I am talking about, and then, when I explain, you probably will not believe me because it will sound so unbelievably old-fashioned and disorderly.

There is this story about a top NASCAR official who threw a party for some of the sport's top drivers several years ago. There were cocktails, and late in the evening when some were well into their cups, two or three of the drivers began questioning why NASCAR did this and why it did not do that. Finally, the official listened until he had enough, at least all he was going to take.

"You guys really don't know as much about racing as you think you do," he says. "Let me explain something to you. Listen carefully, because I will not repeat myself. We have flags, as you know. We have a green flag to tell you when the race begins and to go fast. Then we have a yellow flag to let you know there is a problem, probably a wreck, and you should slow down and get behind the safety car. We have a blue flag with a stripe that we wave to tell you to move over, that a faster car is coming up behind you and you should let it pass. We even have a red flag that we wave when we want to stop the race. It usually means the track is blocked or it is raining too hard to continue.

"We hold up two flags crossed so you will know it is the halfway point of the race. I'm sure you are all familiar with the white flag. It means you only have one more lap to race. And then there is the checkered flag, so you will know when to quit and you can go home. That, gentlemen, leaves us with one flag—the black flag. It means get off the track because we are not going to score you any longer. The president of NASCAR holds that flag every day of every year, and he can wave it when he wants to and point to anyone he so desires. And that, my friends, is the story of NASCAR racing. Don't ever forget it."

The story of racing's most successful sanctioning body has not changed with time. It does not matter what your name is, where you are from, or what you have accomplished. The results are similar: You will obey the rules or look up and see the black flag waving over your head.

NASCAR can be your friend, or the nightmare you will never ride. The sooner you realize this, the better off your career. It's like the fraternity ritual. There is forgiveness, but do not let your candle be blown out too often.

Kevin Harvick's emotions got the best of him at Martinsville, and NASCAR suspended him for one race. *Harold Hinson*

OUT OF THE SHADOWS, INTO THE LIGHT

BY BOB MYERS
From *Circle Track,* October 2002

From Understudy to Leading Man

Kevin Harvick has gone from the background to front-row-center this year, and he's showing some star quality for Richard Childress Racing.

Harold Hinson

"**D**ale Earnhardt was probably the best race car driver there ever is going to be in NASCAR, and nobody will ever replace him. I think we all know that. I would hope that nobody expects me to replace him, because nobody ever will."

Kevin Harvick said that emphatically last February 23, the day car owner Richard Childress announced that the 25-year-old Winston Cup rookie would drive the Chevrolets—a different number and color—the legend left behind when he was killed five days earlier on the final lap of the Daytona 500.

Given Harvick's age, experience, and the circumstances, perhaps no one could have imagined how remarkably he has responded, although Childress never "doubted his ability or hesitated to make the move."

In his first few races, Harvick kept the storied Earnhardt-Childress Racing legacy alive and well, and helped mend thousands of broken hearts. He is building an image for himself in those white No. 29 Goodwrench Monte Carlos much quicker than expected.

"I'll put it this way, I don't know what we'd have done if we hadn't had Kevin Harvick," says Childress, whose cars Earnhardt drove to six of his seven championships and 67 of his 76 victories in 17 consecutive years.

"Everything we do this year we want to do in memory of Dale and try to do some things that aren't normal and that are off the wall," adds Harvick.

Indeed. How about winning at Atlanta, making all the right moves and nipping three-time champion Jeff Gordon by a millisecond for the victory in his third Winston Cup start? No rookie had ever won that quickly. Only five drivers had ever won that soon, the latest in 1963. And how about

ranking 11th in championship points with the victory and three top fives after the season's first 12 races—in spite of missing the Daytona 500?

In the Busch Series Harvick stood second, 19 points behind leader Jeff Green, on the strength of a victory and 11 top 10s after 14 starts in a demanding bid to run the full 33-race schedule in Childress' ACDelco Chevrolets.

Life in a Fish Bowl

The lives of few, if any, drivers have changed as abruptly and drastically as Harvick's. He has

operated in a fish bowl with the stock car world watching since that day in February when he was thrust from the comfortable shadows of obscurity to the bright lights of center stage. That wasn't the way he wanted it. The plan was to make his Winston Cup debut in a third Childress car at Atlanta, the first of seven races this season, and to concentrate on winning the Busch Series championship. But Earnhardt's tragic death changed that and Harvick's life.

Harvick seems to be handling his unexpected transition admirably on and off the track.

"The thing that has impressed me most about Kevin's transition is that he never shows pressure, not on the racetrack, not with the media, and there has to be a lot," says Childress. "He's solid. He's been able to keep the car on the track and competitive. . . . Since he won at Atlanta, I'm not surprised at anything he does on the track because the talent is there."

Obviously another of the gifted freshmen who have followed Jeff Gordon to Winston Cup since 1992, Harvick has given Earnhardt's former team and his legions something to cheer about when they desperately needed a lift. Those who know him best and his associates say his nature is a definite asset. Harvick describes himself as "mellow and laid-back," one who goes week to week, race to race with the flow. He is unusually calm and focused.

"Not much can get me sidetracked," he says. He is smart, knows when to drive aggressively and when to be patient, his crew chief Kevin Hamlin says. In the vernacular of his generation, Harvick is cool.

"A lot of people knew Kevin Harvick, but not hundreds of thousands of them," Harvick says.

His biggest adjustment has been dealing fairly and courteously with fans in greater numbers. He knew that RCR and the Goodwrench car attract a lot of attention that would be magnified by Earnhardt's absence, creating a situation he had not faced. Harvick worried whether Earnhardt's army would adopt him.

"I knew they would turn against me if we ran dead last every week," he says. "The situation could have been a lot worse if we hadn't started out decent and everybody had taken a negative attitude. I could have been the most hated guy in the sport. Thankfully, the fans have taken me in with open arms. They understand that I can't replace Dale and that I'm not trying to."

Gaining Respect

Harvick says his fellow competitors have also been supportive.

"At the first race at Rockingham, Jeff Burton leaned in the car window and said if there was anything he can do, feel free to ask," he says. "Dale Jarrett said the same thing.

Harvick has been especially impressive with the fans and the media, accepting the pressures of both with equal aplomb. *Harold Hinson*

Everybody has been very receptive, and I think they're pretty comfortable racing around us. Mike Skinner [teammate at RCR] and I talk a bit, and that's very positive. Besides Skinner, I don't venture far out of the realm of my team. I just don't have time."

Childress adds, "When the drivers tell you they're comfortable racing with Kevin, you know he's doing things right. Respect on the track is one of the hardest things for a newcomer to gain."

In the midst of a whirlwind of change, Harvick took another major step in life. On February 28, between his first Winston Cup start at Rockingham and the second at Las Vegas, he married DeLana Linville, an attractive blonde from Kernersville, North Carolina, a small town near Winston-Salem. They met at Michigan Speedway in 1999 through Todd Berrier, a friend of DeLana's and Harvick's Busch Series crew chief. They hit it off at a Christmas party they attended that year and haven't been apart since. She is a multiple

blessing. A former public relations rep for Jeff Gordon and Busch champion Randy Lajoie, DeLana understands the off-track workings of NASCAR better than Harvick.

"She is helping me more than anybody can ever imagine," he says of the nicest Christmas present he has received. "She was nervous for the first couple of weeks about how our life has changed, but her reaction is very positive. She's trying to keep control of me and has her hands full."

It was love at second sight for the Harvicks, who reside in the suburbs of Winston-Salem, five minutes from the RCR shops in Welcome.

"When we met, I didn't think much about it," DeLana says. "At the Christmas party, something clicked. I think it was his sense of humor and his sarcastic attitude. We are very much alike. He is sarcasm at its finest and that's the thing that drew us together.

"What you see in Kevin is what you get. He's laid-back and very calm. But when he gets mad, he's very mad. Both of us have a temper, so we

The menacing black No. 3 will likely never be seen again in a NASCAR race, but Harvick is doing a pretty good job of making the white No. 29 into a contender week in and week out. *Nigel Kinrade*

take it in stride. I think my experience in public relations has helped us see things before they happen. I've been able to take a step back and see how the lives of drivers I worked for changed, apply that to our lives, and advise him. That's not to say he will always listen to me, but I definitely have an opinion. This drastic change came suddenly, but we knew we would be in Winston Cup eventually, and I have all the confidence in his ability."

A Go Kart Graduation

Born in Bakersfield, California, December 8, 1975, about six months after Dale Earnhardt drove his first Winston Cup race, Harvick has been racing something for two decades—since he received a go kart for kindergarten graduation. He raced karts on the national level until age 16. He and his father, Mike, a Kern County firefighter who built stock cars as a sideline, built his first late model.

"The first year I wrecked every week," he recalls. But the second year, he won the track championship at Mesa Marin Raceway. Faced with a limited budget, he fared so well that he was able to race late models off his earnings.

Harvick advanced to the NASCAR Craftsman Truck and Winston West series in 1998 with car owner Wayne Spears.

"We ran the first Winston West race at Las Vegas largely to get seat time," Harvick says. "Then we ran two more and were leading the points, so we decided to run the full schedule and won the championship." In the truck series, he finished 17th in points with three top 5s and five top 10s in 26 starts.

Harvick wasn't aware, but Childress, aided by five Winston West races that were televised, was watching him in both series. Given broader TV coverage and the increasing number of young drivers choosing NASCAR, top car owners are actively scouting and recruiting talent at lower levels.

In 1998, Harvick competed in 56 races. That was no big deal. A wrestler in high school, he had developed mental toughness, intensity, strength, and stamina, reflected today by his solid 5-foot, 10-inch, 175-pound frame.

Harvick accepts running the Winston Cup and Busch series—68 points races if he does it—as a challenge. He's more concerned about weather and logistics than physical demands.

"It might take an edge off both cars at times," he says. "But I'm actually excited about it. I probably sound crazy, but that's because people don't fully understand. I've got a lot of people counting on me, but I look at that as support, not pressure. I love being in a car, love to race, love competition. It's my own little world. The best way to get me to do something is to tell me I can't. That fuels the fire in me. I

want everybody to see us on the stage when I say, 'I told you so.'

"I knew coming in that Winston Cup racing is the toughest there is, but I never go into anything with presumptions. If you go into something thinking it's tougher than it is, you're not mentally where you need to be. I just go in, assess the situation, and see where I stand."

The year 2000 was a whirlwind for the 25-year-old Californian. He took over a fallen legend's famous car, got married, and won his first NASCAR Winston Cup event in his third start. *Harold Hinson*

Harvick took a chance and ran low on fuel so that he could win the Tropicana 400 in July 2002. *Nigel Kinrade*

"I knew they [Earnhardt's legion of fans] would turn against me if we ran dead last every week . . . . I could have been the most hated guy in the sport. Thankfully, the fans . . . understand that I can't replace Dale and that I'm not trying to."

—Kevin Harvick

Climbing the Ladder

The Childress connection was made but didn't progress until a truck race at Martinsville in 1999. During the race, Harvick, driving for Liberty Racing, made some gutsy moves and beat and banged on Childress' truck driven by Jay Sauter. They finished 10th and 11th, respectively.

"I had a contract with Liberty, so Childress sent me a message saying he was interested in doing something with me," recalls Harvick. "He wouldn't talk to me until I got a 30-day release from my contract. Fortunately everything worked out." Harvick completed the 1999 truck season with Liberty 12th in points with six top 5s and 11 top 10s.

Switching to the Busch Series in 2000, his first season with Childress, Harvick showcased his talent, earning victories at St. Louis, Bristol, and Memphis to go with 16 top 10s in 31 starts. He finished third in points.

Harvick doesn't recall exactly where and when he first met Dale Earnhardt, except that it was after he joined Childress.

"I was awed," Harvick says. "Hey, this was Dale Earnhardt, the biggest figure in auto racing, the man who was my hero growing up and who my dad admired so much. Now we were on the same team. He was so intimidating that later I didn't want to say anything to him because I thought he might not want to talk to me. I'd just walk up, nudge him, ask how he was doing and go on. I didn't know him as well personally as most of the other guys at RCR."

Apparently, Earnhardt knew Harvick and his ability, though. One time Earnhardt joked that he was going to buy out Harvick's contract with Childress. Harvick took that as a high compliment.

Harvick first worked with Hamlin and his Winston Cup team when he test drove Earnhardt's cars last year at Homestead and Kentucky speedways.

"I was very impressed then and I'm more impressed now," says Hamlin. "He has adapted to the car and to longer races. The first 500-mile race he drove he won. He's focused, not easily shaken, and smart. Kevin's as good as I've seen at this point, though I'm a bit surprised at how quickly he has come along. I'm sure we're going to hit bumps down the road, but we've already been in some tough situations and recovered from them."

Harvick says that being with Hamlin and a championship-caliber team has reduced his learning curve. Working closely with Berrier and the Busch cars has helped Hamlin understand what Harvick likes in his cars. During the winter, Hamlin concentrated on improving Earnhardt's cars and has incorporated changes into Harvick's package. Notebooks on Earnhardt chassis setups are still in use.

Harvick sets high goals but keeps everything in perspective. "We'd like to finish in the top 10 in Winston Cup points and try to win rookie of the year," he says. "We want to win the Busch championship. We know these goals are far-fetched, but we think we can attain them. . . . We wanted to win a [Winston Cup] race for Dale the first year and we did that quicker than expected. It's been the craziest few months of my life. It's pretty cool, but I also understand that there's a realistic factor in here somewhere that has to take place."

PEOPLE'S CHOICE AWARDS 2002:

BIGGEST DISAPPOINTMENT, MOST AGGRESSIVE DRIVER

Kevin Harvick

From *Stock Car Racing*, November 2002

For 2002, Stock Car Racing's *readers selected Kevin Harvick for two seemingly competing awards—Biggest Disappointment and Most Aggressive Driver. Here's the scoop:*

On the surface it appears that these two categories could be linked. Some may blame Kevin Harvick's poor first half of the season on his willingness to see how far he can push his race car. In reality, many more factors conspired to turn last season's rookie sensation into a flunky at times in 2002.

Much was expected of Harvick this season. After taking over Dale Earnhardt's Goodwrench Chevrolet in 2001, Harvick drove to a pair of wins and finished ninth in the Winston Cup point standings.

But the bottom fell out in 2002. In the first 18 races of the season, Harvick finished 25th or worse 11 times. Things got so bad that car owner Richard Childress switched the crews of the No. 31 car of Robby Gordon and Harvick's No. 29 team.

A payoff appeared at Daytona when Harvick won the pole for the Pepsi 400, and finished

that up by winning at Chicago. The verdict is still out on whether 2002 will be considered a huge failure for Harvick, or whether he'll turn the corner enough to salvage a respectable season.

While his performance rises and falls, Harvick's one consistency is his aggressiveness on the racetrack. He's put a fender to nearly everyone in the garage area, building enough of a bad boy reputation that NASCAR parked him for the spring Martinsville race because of his rough driving. "Will trade paint with anybody!" wrote Todd Mangold of Fort Shaw, Montana. Yes, Harvick's had more scrapes than a five-year-old playing on a jungle gym, providing at least a little excitement in a car long known for its intimidating qualities.

Harvick had time to ponder his season when NASCAR suspended him for the spring race at Martinsville. *Jamie Squire/Getty Images*

The 2002 season proved to be a tough one for Harvick. *Harold Hinson*

JIMMIE JOHNSON

5

Born: September 17, 1975

Hometown: El Cajon, California

Height: 5-11

Weight: 175 lbs.

Sponsor	**Lowe's**
Make	**Chevrolet**
Crew Chief	**Chad Knaus**
Owner	**Jeff Gordon/Rick Hendrick**

NASCAR Winston Cup Career Statistics

Year	Races	Wins	Top 5s	Top 10s	Poles	Total Points	Final Standing	Winnings
2001	3	0	0	0	0	210	52	$122,320
2002	36	3	6	21	5	4,600	5	$2,697,702
Totals	39	3	6	21	5	4,800		$2,820,022

Jimmie Johnson prepares to test his Busch car at USA International Speedway. *Dick Kelley*

OFF ROAD AND ON TRACK

BY RON LEMASTERS JR.
From *Stock Car Racing*, December 1999

Jimmie Johnson's Career Starts Going in Circles

Jimmie Johnson raises his arms in triumph after an ASA victory. *ASA photo*

Jimmie Johnson came from the same background as Rick Mears, has the studied polish of Jeff Gordon and Tony Stewart, and has his sights set on a career as a stock car driver.

He's the latest sure thing to come from the fertile mind of Herb Fishel and the talent boffins at GM Motorsports, and he's spent the last year or two making Fishel look like the genius he is thought to be in racing circles.

Ask Johnson who he is, however, and you'll get a different reaction.

"I'm just a 23-year-old kid from Oakland, California," he quips.

While forgiving the young man for modesty, he's quite a bit more than that. He's the future—or at least a part of it—of NASCAR stock car racing.

Since he came to the American Speed Association's ACDelco Challenge Series in 1997 for a three-race stint, he's been one of those drivers everyone watches. Even while blowing off the sand and grit he accumulated after six years in the tough SCORE desert racing series and the now-defunct Mickey Thompson Stadium Off-Road Series, Johnson caught the eye of people who mattered.

One of them was Fishel, always on the lookout for fresh talent he can plug into one of the many General Motors racing programs. With the help of his father, Johnson was taken into the Chevrolet fold while still legally unable to hold a driver's license in some states.

"A lot of people know Herb for keeping an eye out for young drivers, and he's done it so much in the past," Johnson says of Fishel. "He is someone who expressed interest in me when I was 16. He's not someone I speak to every day, but I talk to him a lot. He's so deep into motorsports, he knows what's happening at all times, and he has my best interests at heart. He seems like he's working every day to make sure I'm as strong as I can be, both inside and outside of the car. He's a really unique man. With my upbringing

and background, there've been a few people who have made this possible, and Herb's one of them. If he hadn't, I'd still be sitting at El Cajon, doing what everybody else I graduated high school with is doing."

Fishel found Johnson racing in the stadium off-road series and saw something in the youngster he liked.

"I started out in motocross, but I had one too many broken bones," Johnson says. "My dad, Gary, was into motorcycle racing growing up, so I got involved in that with him. At the same time, when I was getting older, he was a mechanic on a buggy that raced in the Mickey Thompson Stadium Off-Road circuit, and through his connections and his work, he got me into a class called Superlites. He got me in there to a test session for a team sponsored by BF Goodrich Tires. I got started at 15 running the stadium series, and from there Chevrolet picked me up when I was 16, when they were starting to run a second truck in the stadium series."

Grand National Sport Trucks were the cream of the stadium series crop, and a 16-year-old kid driving one of them was certainly a novelty. "They started testing me for the ride, and I got it," Johnson remembers. "When I got involved with Chevrolet, they were interested in looking at and building a future, and I think Herb Fishel probably set that up the most. He's the one who presented me to Chevrolet. He really got the ball rolling at Chevrolet and had a lot of interest in me. I expressed to them where I wanted to go with my racing, and that was stock cars."

Stock car racing is probably one of the tougher divisions in racing to break into these days, with NASCAR having its feeder systems designed to point the best and brightest to its premier divisions—the NASCAR Winston Cup, Busch Grand National, and Craftsman Truck Series.

Even so, ASA racing groomed a number of current Cup and BGN stars including Mark Martin, Rusty Wallace, Kenny Wallace, Ted Musgrave, Dick Trickle, and the late Alan Kulwicki. It also had a hand

in propelling drivers like Darrell Waltrip toward the limelight, even though it was a fledgling series some 30 years ago when Waltrip was on the rise. "That opportunity [to go stock car racing] happened for me in 1997 when I ran three ASA races with Bud Gebben's API team, which is who [1998 series champion] Gary St. Amant drives for," Johnson says. "They tested me and practiced me and took me to my first few races.

"At the same time, Herb Fishel and Chevrolet were discussing with the Herzogs about doing an ASA program and moving into asphalt racing. They've always been a real strong organization in off-road racing, and at that time I was driving their off-road truck. Herb saw them as the team for the future and me as a driver of the future and actually kind of guided us both to where we are now."

Where he is now is the top echelon of the extremely competitive ASA field, and he won his first race in series competition in June at Memphis Motorsports Park in Tennessee.

In five years Johnson hopes to be among the elite in the NASCAR world, despite never having really considered that as an attainable goal growing up.

"I would hope to see myself in Winston Cup, being competitive," Johnson says, pondering what his future holds five years from now. "Dirt racing was everything to me as a kid growing up, and I'd see those NASCAR races on TV and I just didn't think it was possible for me to get there. Now it seems that it's become less of a dream and more of a reality. It's hard for me to figure out how it all happened to start with, but the racer in me—I want to move up.

"We're going to run the full Busch schedule next year, and I think we're going to be competitive there. I've always been able to win races wherever I've raced, and I want to win, not just go there and fill the field. I want to go there and be competitive and run strong. We'll have some maturity with the team, and the Herzogs share some of the same goals I do as far as moving up and growing together. It's a long way to go and we'll see what happens. I just want to win races."

Winning races is what it's all about, and Johnson has adapted well to racing on tracks where the surface doesn't dry up and blow away like it does in the middle of the desert. His transition to the asphalt hasn't been without its worrisome aspects, however.

"Every track and track surface has its own rhythm, and asphalt is all about rhythm," Johnson says. "On the dirt, you've got things changing, as far as the cushion goes and the surface and all the rest. On asphalt, it takes awhile to find that and find it for each track."

The biggest challenge for Johnson was trying to maintain his concentration for three or four hours behind the wheel. "It's really a lot different inside the car, training your brain to be alert for 250 laps," he says, a little wonderingly. "When I ran the desert series, you raced against the clock for 20 hours. The majority of the racing I've done, in the stadium series, has been 15-minute sprint races, and those were the long ones. So to go 300 or 400 laps at a whack was something I had to train myself to do.

"After a pit stop, even if it was the first one, I'd be thinking the race was almost over, even if we had three or four more [stops] to go. Being able to save the equipment, knowing that this might be the last time putting left-side tires on, maybe I'll have another set of rights, and when you spin the left rear tire you're also spinning the rights—just learning about all that. It's been a pretty steep learning curve."

Climbing mountains in stock car racing is much easier if you have someone like Howie Lettow in your pit box. The veteran chief mechanic is the unchallenged star maker in ASA racing, having groomed Musgrave, Bobby Dotter, and several other drivers for future stardom.

Johnson's experience in testing off-road setups and other forms of racing has helped bridge the gap as well.

"I think, with the testing that I've done in off-road tire testing, shock testing, and durability testing on the whole has made me very sensitive to the car," Johnson says. "I'm able to relate things to the car and know exactly what the car needs. I don't know enough about the stock cars yet to know exactly what to do to fix it, but I'm learning that every weekend. I've been able to tell Howie what I'm feeling and we can work on it from there. While he's working on it, he's teaching me what I need to know to fix it."

"Every track and track surface has its own rhythm, and asphalt is all about rhythm."
—Jimmie Johnson

There hasn't been much "fixing" involved in Johnson's ASA career, at least as far as wrecked race cars go. There's a reason for that, Johnson says, and it has to do with a very large rock, a failure in communications, and some Mexican off-road racing fans.

"It was at the Baja 1000, in 1995 or 1996, and I took down the 880-mile marker when I crashed," Johnson reflects with a rueful note in his voice. "I thought I could drive straight through. I was leading the race and I had a problem, threw the power steering belt and the oil pump belt off the truck, then when we tried to start the truck the starter motor was dead. We lost about an hour or so trying to get the truck back on the road. We got it back on the road, and at that point I figured I was out of the race, but I was still charging hard. Little did I know that the other two trucks that had passed me had broken down, which put me back in the lead.

"So I'm charging hard. I'd been driving for 20 hours then, hadn't slept yet. So I dozed off a little bit. I drove into a rainstorm that woke me up, and I was still on the track, but I was coming up on a turn. I was going way too fast for the turn. I tried to get it slowed down, but I knew I was going off the road, so I figured I better go off straight.

"When I plowed through everything, there was a rock the size of a Volkswagen Bug sitting there. I hit the rock and flipped and flipped. I'm down at the bottom of this little sand wash. You won't believe this, but there were about 100 Mexicans at the bottom of this wash, with bonfires and their wives and everything, watching the race. A lot of times the people who watch the race like that go out and pull markers down and wait to see a crash.

"Well, they got to see their crash. I spent two days with those guys until the communication went to my crew guys. My chase truck had a problem and was broken down. By the time the chase truck for my teammate, Larry Raglund, got to me, it was almost two days later."

During that time Johnson did some serious ruminating on how the situation had come to pass.

"I had a lot of time to sit there and reflect," he says. "I drove for John Nelson, and John always wanted you to run hard.

"He really pushed me to charge hard in the stadium stuff. I was 18 years old, wound up, ready to charge hard, and I got into a desert truck. You really have to have some experience to race those. You race the clock; it's an endurance race. After that crash, I really started reflecting on my style. Since that crash—and I raced two more years of off-road—I never had that truck upside down, and I've never torn anything up in stock cars."

Despite that, Johnson still considers himself an aggressive driver. "Ever since then I've been on the right side of the aggressive line, where before I crossed it quite frequently and had been lucky enough to save it. But I think I've gotten a little older and a little more mature. I still feel I'm pretty aggressive."

Training for the oval tracks in the desert has helped drivers like Indianapolis 500 winners Rick Mears and Parnelli Jones, and it has helped Johnson in certain ways, too.

"I think it's easier for a dirt racer to go race on asphalt than it is the other way around," he says. "In dirt racing, you learn to drive a car comfortably on the edge all the time. When you get in an asphalt car, if you adjust your style enough, driving that car properly, when you get in situations it doesn't bother you that much, and you can drive that way every lap. I can see why the dirt helps you."

What he couldn't prepare for, despite the fact he was racing in the middle of the desert, was the heat inside a stock car.

"In desert racing you never had a windshield, so you always had fresh air blowing across you," says Johnson. "Even out in the desert in the summer, like in Barstow, California, when it's 115 degrees out, when you're in the truck and the truck's moving, you're relatively cool. I'm hotter in the ASA car on a 50-degree night than I ever was in the 115-degree weather in the middle of the desert, so I've had to adjust to the heat. As hot as temperatures are in the Midwest with the humidity, I try to run in the middle of the day, throw on a sweatshirt and sweatpants, and get used to it that way."

One thing Johnson, like any other stadium racer, doesn't have to adapt to as much as pure desert racers is traffic. It does take a little getting used to, but Johnson has a fix on it.

"The stadium racing I did is sort of like road course racing where you could set somebody up and you'd have a strong section of the track to pass them," he says. "In stock cars, you're always turning left, and it's really the same at either end. Learning how to pass in a stock car was difficult, but as far as running in traffic, I was used to that from my stadium experience. That's one thing I didn't quite care much for, racing in the desert. You'd chase somebody's dust cloud, bust through it, tap him once or twice, he'd move over and you'd go on. You never really raced anybody for anything. That's part of what my problem was in the desert, too. I'd chase all the dust clouds and wouldn't drive my own race."

Driving his own race will come second soon to driving his career. He will have crew chief Tony Liberati in his corner next season. He'll also have a familiar face driving the transporter.

"My parents [father, Gary, and mother, Cathy] are moving to Charlotte soon," Johnson says. "My dad's going to drive the Busch hauler for us next year."

The elder Johnson has had a profound effect on his son's career, pushing hard to get him a ride with Jeff Bennett's Superlites team. "My dad drives the West Coast trailer for BF Goodrich, and Dan Newsome from BF Goodrich first gave me a chance to drive in Superlites with a five-car team sponsored by Nature's Recipe Pet Food," says Jimmie. "Jeff Bennett owned the team, and Dan Newsome really leaned on Jeff to get me the ride. Well, my dad really pressured Dan to pressure Jeff Bennett."

It's a long way from the old stadium course at the L.A. Coliseum to the shining lights of Daytona, Charlotte, and Texas, but it won't be too long a run for the 23-year-old from Oakland, California.

He's been racing against the clock all his life, and it stands to reason he'll beat the clock to his ultimate goal of NASCAR Winston Cup racing.

NO MORE HEADACHES

BY JIMMIE JOHNSON
From *Stock Car Racing*, March 2001

It's one thing to be good and get noticed by important people. It's another to have the next two years mapped out for you with the likes of Jeff Gordon and Hendrick Motorsports. Toward the end of last season, not only did Jimmie Johnson add to an already great Busch Grand National deal with Herzog/Excedrin Racing for this year, he was personally chosen by Jeff Gordon to drive a Hendrick Winston Cup car in 2002. Now, life in NASCAR for the likeable Johnson is without the usual headaches.

Johnson eagerly anticipates his move up to Winston Cup. *SCR Archives*

There's definitely a lot going on. I was just thinking back where I was a year ago at this time. We had just run five Busch races and were looking forward to the 2000 season but didn't know what to expect. It seems like an eternity has gone by, but it's really only been about 12 months. I feel real lucky. I've kind of been saying to people that I've got the yellow brick road laid out in front of me, and I've just got to stroll on down it.

Jeff Gordon's been somebody I've always been able to just go up and talk to and been really approachable. At Michigan, I went to him for advice on some opportunities that were being presented to me. And through that conversation with him, he had mentioned there might be some changes coming at Hendrick Motorsports. There might be something where I would fit in the program. That led to some discussions with Rick Hendrick and with Jeff. Shortly thereafter, they had an offer for me on the table that was a dream come true—really.

They're building a new 85,000-square-foot facility at the current complex. Jeff's going to be part owner in the program, and he's in the No. 24. So they're going to put both teams in-house in the same building, and Jeff's going to move his licensing company in-house and have everything there at Hendrick Motorsports.

They're going to utilize me in a lot of the tests. Simple functions tests—motor testing, brake testing, all that kind of stuff that they don't want to trouble their drivers with. You know, stuff that drives them crazy but stuff I'm really excited to do. I just need to get experience in a [Winston] Cup car and on these tracks. And I've got an awesome Busch program to give me more experience as well.

Hendrick is working real hard to help our Busch program with some added help from the Herzogs. We just came off our rookie year finishing 10th—an exceptional year. We've got a commitment from Excedrin to run the Busch Series for this year. So we kind of all feel we're at the same level—looking forward to the same things. There were some hard times here, getting going with this decision, but everybody knew that this was something I couldn't turn down.

And my owners, Stan, Randy, and Bill Herzog, as sad as they were because they wanted to move onto Cup together, they knew this was an opportunity of a lifetime. They've been like family to me for the last five years, taking me through racing around tires in the dirt to making my dreams come true in stock car racing.

There's been a lot of times where I thought I was crazy, sacrificing even from back in high school. But for some reason in the back of my head, I just was confident that things would work out. And they have.

I've been able to chase my dreams and make all those sacrifices pay off. I was worried at the time: Boy, if racing doesn't work out, what am I going to have? If you just work hard enough at it, and you're a good person, well, good things happen to good people. That's what I pride myself on, and it's all turned out. So, I'm really looking forward to this year and not having to worry about anything—just drive race cars.

A ROOKIE NO MORE

BY RON LEMASTERS JR.
From *Circle Track*, June 2001

Jimmie Johnson Plans to Make the Most of His Sophomore Season in NASCAR's Busch Series

Johnson (92) had high hopes for 2001, beginning with new sponsorship from Excedrin. He was also pointing toward his rookie season in Winston Cup the next season with Hendrick Motorsports. *Sam Sharpe*

Jimmie Johnson is something of a prodigy. At the ripe old age of 25, he has been a motorcycle racing wunderkind, an off-road racing champion, rookie of the year in the American Speed Association, and one of the brightest youngsters to come around since Jeff Gordon first traded top wings for fenders.

As a matter of fact, Johnson's precociousness attracted the attention of the three-time Winston Cup champion last year—enough so that Johnson's maiden venture into the major-league series in 2002 will be run out of Gordon's shops at the massive Hendrick Motorsports complex near Lowe's Motor Speedway.

Last year, however, Johnson was the greenest of rookies on the NASCAR Busch Grand National Series. Going into the season, he hadn't even seen, let alone raced on, some of the tracks on the BGN schedule. Las Vegas Motor Speedway was one of those he'd never seen, but he did recognize the area.

"I raced all around the desert outside of there," he cracked one day last year. "So, I guess you could say I have raced in Las Vegas."

Despite being a very young stock car driver on a team making the jump from ASA to the Busch Series, Johnson and crew chief Tony Liberati fashioned a second-half run that saw them place tenth in the final standings. It is this string of solid performances that

leaves Johnson with the idea that he and his Excedrin-sponsored Herzog Motorsports team can be contenders from the get-go this season.

"In one respect, we didn't want to stop racing last year because we were really starting to hit our stride," Johnson says. "But at the same time, now we all get to start over on a clean sheet of paper and go after the point situation again with that rhythm we had and the confidence and the feeling that we are able to be a contender week in and week out.

"I'm just looking to get started where we left off, and hopefully we can start running in the top 10 consistently like we did at the end of last year," he continued. "Then we need to start knocking down those top 5s, and once that comes, we'll be ready to win some races."

The 2000 season didn't start off exactly as Johnson, Liberati, and the Herzogs wanted—they missed the season opener at Daytona. That, Johnson explains, was as much a matter of expectations set too high as anything else. This season, if anything, the expectations are just as grand. The difference comes from having a season under his belt.

"I hope I'm not thinking too high again," he laughed. "We got off to kind of a slow start by missing Daytona last year and picked up our momentum really about the midpoint of the year. We were able to come back to tenth in the points. Realistically, I think if we start where we left off last year, we would be a top five team in the points and maybe a long shot for the championship."

That's a pretty bold prediction for a second-year team with a new sponsor, but Johnson has a precedent.

"I've been known during the off-season to do this transformation, where everything finally has a chance to soak in," he says. "I think about racing so much, there really hasn't been an off-season yet. I'm thinking of tracks and what we did and going through my notes and setups. In ASA it worked this way. We came out of the box the next season and sat on the front row, and we were competitive immediately. I'm hoping that takes place again, and we have a shot at the championship."

The guesswork, as far as never having seen some of the places he'll race this year, has been removed.

Johnson and Liberati found a way to combat the driver's relative lack of experience, and it worked well during their second-half surge.

"At first, Tony was used to being with an experienced driver who could unload, come off the truck, and cut a qualifying lap," Johnson says. "We tried that at the beginning, but I wasn't at that point to be able to cut a lap first time out because I'd never been there. What we started to learn to do, and fell into a really good rhythm with, was to kind of sacrifice that first set of tires. We're only given two sets of tires for practice, and that first set, we decided, was to let me go out and run five laps at a time to try and find my way around the track and make sure

Many Busch Series venues were new to Johnson during his rookie season. *Sam Sharpe*

I was in the right spot. Then we'd spend the majority of practice getting me seat time and making small adjustments to the car. Then toward the end of practice, we'd stick the second set of tires on the car, make a qualifying run, and find out where we were. We found a lot more success in doing that instead of trying to unload and go fast at the beginning. It made me drive the track wrong and put too much pressure on us right off the bat. Going into this year, I've at least been to these places once and I'm hoping to speed that process up."

Asked what his first piece of advice to a first-year participant in the Busch Series would be, Johnson went the basic route.

"The advice I would give to a young driver is to just be patient," he says. "There isn't anything that gets a driver ready for Busch Grand National racing besides Busch Grand National racing. ARCA, ASA, trucks, any of that stuff is just a totally different animal. It's not hard to get within a half-second, but to get those last few tenths . . . it just takes time. It takes time for you as a driver to learn those little feelings. The only way you work through all those feelings and know what makes the car faster and what makes it out of control is just with seat time. That's the biggest thing I had to go through.

"My desire and ambition, and those of my crew chief and the Herzogs, was so high. We thought we were going to be able to overcome not having a lot of experience. We did a lot in a short period of time, but man that was a hard first half of the year. We were beating our heads against the wall, wondering, 'Why are we not up front? We know that's where we need to be.' It just took some time."

FROM THE DESERT TO DAYTONA

BY BOB MYERS
From *Circle Track,* May 2002

Jimmie Johnson Is the Latest Young

Talent to Climb the Mountain to NASCAR's Top Division

Johnson teamed with four-time NASCAR Winston Cup champion Jeff Gordon and legendary team owner Rick Hendrick for his rookie season in NASCAR's top division. *CT Archives*

Jimmie Johnson has to pinch himself to make sure he's in the real world.

Johnson, a blue-chip rookie, began his first full NASCAR Winston Cup season in February driving the No. 48 Chevrolet for a new Hendrick Motorsports team co-owned by Jeff Gordon and Rick Hendrick and sponsored by Lowe's Home Improvement Warehouse.

Most rookies could only fantasize about having four-time and reigning Winston Cup champion Gordon as a teammate and Hendrick as an owner, plus the vast resources of Hendrick Motorsports at their disposal. Hendrick's multiple teams have won five Winston Cup and three Craftsman Truck Series titles in the past eight years.

That Johnson signed his Winston Cup pact in September 2000 is all that really matters now, but how the deal came about is one for Ripley's.

For the past two seasons Johnson drove Chevrolets for Herzog Motorsports in the NASCAR Busch Grand National Series. In July 2000, Alltel, the team's sponsor,

announced it would not return in 2001. As a result, word traveled fast that Johnson might be available at the end of the season if no sponsor was signed. He began to receive a surprising number of overtures from Winston Cup, Busch, and truck series owners.

Though Herzog eventually signed Excedrin as sponsor for 2001, the uncertainty during the interim weighed heavily on Johnson. What should he do, and how should he handle his situation? All he knew for sure is that if forced to make a change, he would stick with Chevrolet. He first hooked up with Chevrolet when he was 16. Herb Fishel, General Motors' global racing chief, helped steer his career.

A Crazy Idea

Johnson had what he calls a "crazy idea." Why not seek advice? How about Jeff Gordon, who had skyrocketed to fame and fortune and seemed to have done everything right, on and off the track?

Johnson didn't know Gordon beyond a hello. That was enough. At the drivers' meeting before the Busch

race at Michigan Speedway in August 2000, someone sitting behind Johnson grabbed him by the shoulders and said "Hello." It was Gordon, who competed in selected Busch races. Johnson had been trying unsuccessfully to work up enough nerve to ask Gordon for a few minutes of his time. This was his break.

Johnson asked Gordon to see him, and Gordon invited him to his hauler after the meeting. Johnson told Gordon he was seeking advice, but Gordon did most of the talking. To Johnson's utter surprise, Gordon told him that he and Hendrick were interested in him possibly driving for them down the road, and that Hendrick Motorsports planned to add a fourth Winston Cup team to be housed in a new facility with Gordon's four-time champion team: two cars, one team. Gordon went on and on, Johnson says, adding that he didn't want to build Johnson's hopes too high, but advised him to "hang tight."

Johnson was incredulous. "I can't describe my feelings when I walked out of that hauler," he says. "I had gone in there confused, wondering, and searching for advice and had come out with the possibility of a ride with Jeff Gordon and Rick Hendrick. I was simply trying to look ahead, be smart at a young age, and make sure I was going to have a ride in 2001. I wanted to stay with the Herzogs, but if anything happened to the team, I had to be prepared."

Not incidentally, Johnson beat his future boss in the race, finishing sixth, Gordon seventh.

Johnson had met Rick Hendrick at a Chevrolet function some six years earlier. Johnson and Hendrick's son, Ricky, a promising young driver who advanced from Craftsman trucks to Busch this year, are friends who had met through racing. Johnson knew that Fishel in the past had spoken highly of him to Rick Hendrick, but they had said nothing to Johnson about a possible ride.

Gordon promptly informed Hendrick of his conversation with Johnson, and they decided to go after him immediately. In about a month, Johnson autographed the contract. In fact, his signing actually accelerated plans to get the new team on track for the full 2002 schedule.

Living in the Moment

"The timing wasn't exactly right for us, but we were so impressed with Jimmie we needed to get him before somebody else did," Hendrick says. "If you wait around when you see a guy who seems to have it all, the whole package, it's too late.

"It was much the same with signing Jeff [in 1992]. We saw the talent first and then built around him. Jimmie is the reason we sped up this deal. . . . He's very talented and sharp, his communication skills and feedback are incredible, and he's just a great individual. Chemistry has developed between him and Jeff over the past year, and I think what Jeff can offer as his teammate is a huge asset. Their driving styles are about the same. We're very fortunate to have Jimmie in the Hendrick stable. He's an excellent fit. I think he is one of the best, if not the best, to come along in a long time."

Gordon says Johnson wasn't hired because there was no one else available; he was the right man for the job. "I raced with Jimmie some in the Busch series, and I've gotten to know him personally," says Gordon, listed as the team's official owner. "Not only am I very impressed with his talent, but the way he handles himself with sponsors, media, and fans. Today's Winston Cup driver has to have the whole package, and that's hard to find. I am very excited about what we have found in Jimmie. He is a young and aggressive driver and gets the most out of his car."

At 5 feet, 11 inches and 175 pounds, Johnson is physically larger than Gordon, but their clean-cut appearance, some of their features, and their engaging personalities are similar. They're both California natives, Johnson hailing from El Cajon and Gordon from Mission Viejo. Johnson is 26 years old; Gordon is 30. Gordon has won 58 Winston Cup races, Johnson none.

A Head Start

With the addition of bright, young crew chief Chad Knaus, Johnson believes he and his team have a head start on the new season. He made his Winston Cup debut bittersweet because he ran impressively in the top four before making a rookie mistake and crashing

In two seasons with Herzog Motorsports, Johnson finished in the top 10 in points both years and gave the team its first Busch Series victory in the inaugural race at Chicagoland Speedway. *Harold Hinson*

out at Charlotte in October and also raced at Homestead-Miami and Atlanta.

"We've had more than a year to build equipment and shop relationships with all the people involved," Johnson says. Even though his debut in the UAW-GM 500 ended prematurely with disappointment, Johnson feels, based on overall performance, ". . . that I made the transition to Winston Cup and that I am ready."

Johnson's initial objective this year was to make the field for the first four races because going in there are no owner's points toward provisional starts. "From there, I just want to earn the respect of these guys," he says ". . . I want to show them that they can race side-by-side with me and have confidence in my ability. Looking at what past rookies have done—Earnhardt Jr., Matt Kenseth, Tony Stewart, and Kevin Harvick—I think I will have every opportunity to be as successful. I'd certainly like to top Harvick's two wins [in 2001]."

"If Jimmie is competitive, qualifies in the top 20, and shows he has the potential to win, that's as much as I'd expect the first year," adds Hendrick. Johnson has earned a crack at stock car racing's premier series. He raced through the minor leagues on motorcycles and in off-road buggies and trucks and American Speed Association (ASA) and NASCAR Busch Series stockers.

Given that he has raced stock cars for only four years, his progress has been rapid. Johnson joined Herzog Motorsports, led by Bill Herzog and his sons, Stan and Randy, in 1996 and drove their off-road trucks for two seasons. Johnson, with the blessings of Fishel and Chevrolet, moved with the Herzogs to ASA stockers in 1998, purchasing a Milwaukee-based team.

Johnson knew nothing about stock cars. He moved his residence to Milwaukee to spend more time with crew chief Howie Lettow, a top ASA wrench whose students include Mark Martin, Ted Musgrave, and the late Winston Cup champion Alan Kulwicki. "The transition was huge for me," Johnson says. "I give Lettow all the credit for bridging the gap and teaching me the basics. He could explain complicated things so simply. From there, I was able to grow."

In the ASA, Johnson won two races and finished fourth and a close second in the championship standings. While maintaining a full ASA schedule, Johnson broke into NASCAR in 1998 with three Busch series starts in Herzog Chevrolets. Led by crew chief Tony Liberati, a former Winston Cup mechanic and car chief, he made five Busch starts in 1999, with a best finish of seventh.

Johnson's Busch numbers aren't as flashy as others who have advanced to Winston Cup, but he is pleased with his progress. In 2000, he posted six top 10s and finished tenth in points in 31 starts. Last year, he won for the first time, the inaugural Busch race at the new Chicagoland Speedway, logged four top 5s, nine top 10s, and ranked eighth in points after 30 starts.

"If I had been told when I left ASA that I would finish tenth in points the first year in Busch and the second season win a race and finish in the top 10 again, I'd have said, 'Shoot, I'll take that,'" Johnson

says. "Winning the first race at Chicagoland was awesome. We didn't back into it. We raced hard. We were fortunate to hold off Ryan Newman at the end because he has been incredible in Penske [South] equipment. I am so happy to get the first Busch win for the Herzogs, who have put a lot into me in six years, and for Tony. I feel bad about leaving, but they understand."

Liberati, who remains at Herzog Motorsports to lead driver Andy Houston this season, believes Johnson is ready for the big league. "He did fine in ASA and Busch," says Liberati, who has worked in Winston Cup seven years. "Tony Stewart didn't win a Busch race, but he set the Winston Cup series on fire as a rookie. Everything is there for Jimmie to be as good as some of the other rookies, to do what Stewart and Harvick did their first year."

From the Desert to Daytona

Johnson didn't get from his 50cc Suzuki bike at age five to Hendrick Motorsports by himself, as his gratitude to the Herzogs and Liberati attests. He grew up in motorcycle racing, the thing to do in El Cajon at the time, admiring and emulating Rick Johnson (no relation), a seven-time motocross champion. Interestingly enough, Rick Johnson replaced Jimmie as Herzog's ASA driver when Jimmie left for the Busch Series. Jimmie's father, Gary, got him onto motorcycles and, challenged by broken bones and medical

bills, off of them into cars and trucks, much to mom Cathy's relief.

Car owner Jeff Bennett gave Johnson his first ride in a race car—a buggy in the Mickey Thompson Stadium Off-Road Series. That led to his alliance with Fishel and Chevrolet. He honed his driving skills in desert and stadium trucks owned by Jon Nelson and his father, Pops. In the off-road and stadium series, Johnson won more than 25 races and, including motorcycles, six championships.

With age and experience, Johnson has matured. "I try to race with my brain instead of my feet," he says. "I tore up a lot of off-road equipment because I was young and wide open. I hope I've gotten a lot of that out of my system. I seem to have more control now. There's lots of pressure in Winston Cup, but I think it will be fun."

Johnson's girlfriend, Jessica Bergendahl of Long Beach, California, lends support while he chases his dream. They met at a Christmas party six years ago. Johnson finally got a date with her after nine months of rejection and that led to a "great relationship." "Jessica is a beautiful blonde-haired California girl just like you would imagine," says Johnson. "She baby-sits me with genuine support and love. She's never tried to slow me down from what I want to do. She's working on a master's degree in psychology and has things she wants to do. Someday I'll get married. It's important to have that stability in life."

Away from the track, Johnson, who has a home on Lake Norman, an exclusive Winston Cup bedroom community near Mooresville, North Carolina, enjoys water sports. He spends as much time as his schedule allows with Jessica and his family. His parents have relocated to Mooresville and his dad drives Johnson's motor home to races. He has two younger brothers, Jarit, 22, and Jesse, 12.

Johnson's tastes include steak and seafood dinners with a glass of wine and alternative rock and country music. He likes to dance, though he is smoother on wheels, he says. He follows the stock market and tries to understand the oft-disturbing news of the world. His TV plays a lot just for the noise.

Johnson has been reading books, some on religion to strengthen his faith, not just because his good friend and fellow driver Blaise Alexander was killed in an ARCA race at Lowe's Motor Speedway the night of Winston Cup qualifying in October. "It was something I felt inside, and Jessica and I have started growing together," Johnson says. "I think all of us were put here for a reason. It has helped me through the loss of Blaise, another good friend in Wisconsin, and my grandparents. That was hard to grasp, but I'm a lot stronger now. It's made me smile about Blaise instead of being so sad for so long. I think he's in a better place, served his purpose here, and it was time for him to move on."

Johnson thought little of a career in NASCAR or Winston Cup until his late teens. He seriously considered Indy cars. As a youth, he was a big fan of three-time Winston Cup champion Cale Yarborough. "Cale was awesome," he says. "He was sponsored by Hardees. When we traveled and stopped at one of the restaurants, I always expected Cale to be there, but he never was." Johnson never met Yarborough, or fallen heroes Davey Allison and Dale Earnhardt. He has met and spent time with another hero, Bobby Allison, over the past two years. "I met a lot of the Winston Cup guys for the first time at my first race," he says.

But meeting Jeff Gordon changed Jimmie Johnson's life, just how much is yet to be determined. And there is no doubt about who is his biggest hero.

Johnson's Lowe's Home Improvement Warehouse Chevrolet carried a slightly different paint scheme than it did in 2001. *Jeff Huneycutt*

COOL, CONFIDENT, AND CASHING IN

BY LARRY COTHREN
From *Stock Car Racing*, October 2002

Young Drivers Work Some Marketing Magic and Race All the Way to the Bank

Johnson joined Kurt Busch, Ryan Newman, Kevin Harvick, and Dale Earnhardt Jr. among those drivers who made waves in the world of racing in 2002. *Nigel Kinrade*

> "Obviously we've all been given great opportunities and great equipment. A few of us have some great coaches to learn from, so we're all making the most of it."
>
> —Jimmie Johnson

Bill Elliott can look back to his successful run for the Winston Million in 1985 as a time of change during his racing career. The Elliott clan, Bill and brothers, Ernie and Dan, claimed R. J. Reynolds' million-dollar bonus that year by winning three of four designated races, but it wasn't simply the money that changed the way the Elliotts operated. Unprecedented attention from the media began to cut deeply into Elliott's time spent working on his car that season. The crush became so bad that Elliott needed armed guards in order to work on his record-setting Thunderbird.

You won't find many Winston Cup drivers today who actually work on their cars, but even more attention is focused on the sport. Instead of preventing drivers from tuning their engines or crawling under their cars to adjust the suspension—as Elliott and a few drivers still did in the mid-1980s—the demands of the sport today might force a driver to be late for a personal appearance, a television interview, or a commercial shoot.

In a world of stock car racing where corporations once feared to tread, marketing terms such as "demographics" and "target audience" are now part of the Sunday afternoon vernacular. And nowhere is marketing success more prevalent than in the wave of young drivers who have swept to the forefront of NASCAR.

"When we came into this deal, we didn't have any money," Elliott says. "I don't take that as being a negative. I learned what I had to learn during my era. I've been able to adapt throughout the years. I'm very happy today. That's evolution. Guys are going to come in here and push you out. That's part of it. That's the part we've got to understand."

Quick Kids

The current crop of young drivers making waves in the sport—Dale Earnhardt Jr., Elliott Sadler, Kevin Harvick, Kurt Busch, Jimmie Johnson, Ryan Newman, and Casey Atwood, who range from 28- to 22-years old—have become familiar to even casual fans of the sport. Over the past decade, a firm foundation for their success has been put in place.

Tony Stewart actually redefined rookie success in 1999 when he won a record three races and finished fourth in Winston Cup points for Joe Gibbs Racing. The trend toward young, successful drivers goes back even further, though, to Jeff Gordon's success as a 22-year-old in 1993, when he was rookie of the year. He won twice the next year and new fans began to flock to the sport because of Gordon. In terms of marketing and appeal to younger, never-before-reached markets, Earnhardt Jr. has picked up where Gordon left off and single-handedly redefined success in the marketplace.

Youthful vigor on the track hasn't equated to positive PR off the track, however. Two of the most successful rookies ever in NASCAR, Stewart and Harvick, have been two of the most volatile drivers off the track. Harvick, who won twice, finished ninth in

"There are probably a lot of fathers today coaching their kids in go kart racing and mini-sprints rather than Little League."

—Tom Cotter,
motorsports marketing executive

points, and was Winston Cup Rookie of the Year in 2001, has had several well-documented flare-ups this season, as Stewart did in 2001.

This season a young, articulate, well-mannered driver has combined the best of both worlds. Jimmie Johnson is not only saying and doing the right things off the track, he's winning on the track at a pace ahead of even Stewart's rookie campaign. By the Pepsi 400 at Daytona, the midpoint of the season, Johnson had won two races and was fourth in points.

Johnson personifies the young, aggressive, winning driver that teams have searched for since Gordon lowered the bar in terms of when to expect success in the sport. For his sponsor, Lowe's, which joined Hendrick Motorsports at the beginning of this season, Johnson's ability to win quickly has meant a reversal of fortunes. The company spent five seasons as a sponsor before reaching victory lane in a Winston Cup point race with Richard Childress Racing and driver Robby Gordon in last season's finale at New Hampshire. Lowe's languished in the shadows of NASCAR success while rival Home Depot hit the jackpot in 1999 with Gibbs and Stewart, a combination that produced 12 wins in three seasons.

Getting Noticed

There are parallels between Johnson's success this season and Stewart's in 1999: Both drivers moved to the Winston Cup series after having modest success in the Busch Series, both came from outside the NASCAR realm—Stewart, an Indiana native, came from open-wheel racing, and Johnson, a Californian, came from off-road racing—and both landed with established Winston Cup teams. Their personalities, however, differ as much as the fiery orange and placid blue that make up the primary colors of their respective sponsors.

Home Depot's Hugh Miskel, director of sales development, says Stewart's occasional public relations problems are outweighed by the benefits of exposure gained by the company. "You sort of have the

Dale Earnhardt Jr. (left) won twice during his rookie year, while Kurt Busch didn't reach victory lane until his sophomore season. *Harold Hinson*

philosophy that if you finish in first or in flames, as long as they're talking about you on Monday morning at the water cooler, you have to view it as a success," says Miskel.

Earning exposure is the name of the game in marketing. When a company is shelling out $10 million or more per year in sponsorship money, getting noticed is of primary concern. Getting noticed in victory lane is the ultimate goal. Companies look for drivers who can perform on the track and behave like a gentleman away from it. Still, young drivers are largely unproven in the major leagues, sometimes with little or no success in a stock car, and even less experience facing a media swarm.

"First, you don't know what they can really do in the Cup series, in the top series," says Max Muhleman, president of IMG/Muhleman Marketing. "Then they have their own personal risks. Some of the

Johnson's pole-winning run for the 2002 Daytona 500 was an early highlight for the rookie driver.
Sam Sharpe

sors relied on other mechanisms of evaluation. In aligning with Joe Gibbs Racing and Stewart, Home Depot relied on Gibbs' reputation for success and his ability to deal with people. Lowe's used the same strategy with Hendrick Motorsports and Johnson, relying on Jeff Gordon's assessment of Johnson.

While those two situations paid off quite well, with two of the top seasons ever by Winston Cup rookies, many risks remain in choosing unproven stock car drivers. For every Johnson there's a Jason Leffler, who dropped back to the NASCAR Craftsman Truck Series this year after spending an unsuccessful 2001 in Winston Cup with Ganassi Racing. For every Stewart, there's a Scott Pruett, a road-racing veteran who was unsuccessful in his attempt to cross over to stock car racing with Cal Wells in 2000.

Miskel insists that Home Depot's primary motivation to get involved in NASCAR came from the company's employees, and the company has used its association with Gibbs and Stewart as a tool to boost morale internally while at the same time giving employees common ground with customers. The impact, buoyed by Stewart's success, has been better than expected.

"I think there is some uncertainty going into any sponsorship as far as what the return is going to be," says Miskel. "The early success of the program exceeded our expectations and has created a very positive umbrella effect over the entire program, which is going to allow it to do more both internally and externally, whether it's [NASCAR] products in our stores or entertainment of customers. And that has and can have a very positive effect on our business overall. I think the outlook for us is very positive, because the on-track performance has been a bonus to everything else we've put in place. . . . It has only enhanced everything we've done."

Bucking Tradition

NASCAR drivers have traditionally been considered in their prime when they reach their mid-30s. So, how can a driver such as a Jimmie Johnson or a Tony Stewart not only win early but also be consistently competitive, while some of the sport's top names didn't find consistent success until later in their careers? Primarily, the new guys are getting into good equipment quicker than did their predecessors, who had to pay their dues before getting an opportunity in a top car. And with the number of quality sponsors involved today—sponsors who provide the money for successful ventures—there are simply more good cars out there.

Then there's the Gordon factor. Gordon's early success—he was Winston Cup champion soon after turning 24—changed the dynamics of the sport, paving the way for young guys who've followed. With more quality rides available, and with team owners more willing to take a chance on a young driver, due to Gordon's success, the result is more young drivers in the limelight.

"Virtually every sponsor is hoping to find the next

risks are just like those we see in other major league sports, frankly, where a lot more money than they've ever had before comes their way, and they have 'how-do-they-behave' risks. The other risk, of course, is the one of not being able to do what you expect them to do."

Stewart and Johnson did nothing to set themselves apart in the Busch Series, with Stewart going winless and Johnson winning just once, so both spon-

Jeff Gordon," says Tom Cotter, managing director of CMI Cotter Group, a marketing firm with close ties to the sport. "Because of his success we're seeing a lot more young guys going for it. There are probably a lot of fathers today coaching their kids in go kart racing and mini-sprints rather than Little League."

As the Jeff Gordons and Jimmie Johnsons and Tony Stewarts reach victory lane, NASCAR's fan base expands into new territory. While Major League Baseball considers contraction and the NBA comes to grips with a future without Michael Jordan, major league stock car racing is reaching an unprecedented number of households, thanks primarily to a billion-dollar television package now in its second year and, yes, thanks to a new wave of young drivers.

Even *Sports Illustrated* took notice earlier this year, putting Dale Earnhardt Jr. on its cover, an undeniably rare placement for a NASCAR driver. With Earnhardt Jr. reaching the pages of *People* magazine and appearing on MTV, and with Gordon making appearances on popular talk shows, NASCAR has become mainstream in America, appealing to a cross section of fans, especially young ones. A Britney Spears movie based on NASCAR is even in the works.

"NASCAR had traditionally appealed to older adults, say from the late 20s, maybe 30 on up," says Cotter. "But there's a whole huge marketing segment of people who have billions of dollars of marketing power, billions of dollars of buying power; NASCAR has not been at the top of the mind with those people. Having a driver like Jeff Gordon, who appears on the cover of magazines they may read, or more lately Dale Earnhardt Jr., who is appearing on everything that's hip, that's attracting a lot more media attention in the media of a particular demographic type. It's hard to escape NASCAR. That's how you breed new blood to take over the reins of fandom in this sport."

As the fan base grows, the sport benefits in several ways. "The interesting thing is both of the cola companies are in it and they have one of the youngest demo skews of anybody," Muhleman says. "They're interested in demographics down to 12 years old, which is a lot younger than motor oil or something like that. As the demographics improve, the sponsor net gets wider."

The End Result

Sponsors, meanwhile, have become increasingly impatient in recent seasons, as the demand to win correlates directly with the amount of money spent. "Silly Season," NASCAR's annual period of driver changes and rumors of driver changes, experienced a spring renewal this year, earlier than ever before, primarily because of impatient sponsors and the pressures team owners face.

"There seems to be a lot more immediacy now," says Cotter. "The price of sponsorship has gone up so dramatically in recent years [that] there is not as much patience to wait for a program to come around and start showing benefits and increasing sales of whatever product a company has.

"There used to be, 'Plant the seed and we'll wait for sales to rise.' Now it's much more immediate: 'We want to start seeing increased sales over the next two quarters,' and there has to be measurement mechanisms put in place. The reason for that is racing has gotten expensive. It's on the radar charts now, not as just throwing away a couple of million dollars and saying, 'We'll see what happens.'"

It remains to be seen whether the current youth movement will be a lasting trend or a passing phenomenon; whether twenty-something drivers will be leading the sport or merely following experienced veterans. In every other major sport, after all, athletes typically are most productive before age 35. Should stock car racing be any different?

Of the 19 different winners last season, five were 30 or younger, and five of 11 winners were 31 or younger during the first half of this season. Second-year driver Kurt Busch was 23 when he won at Bristol during March of this year, joining Johnson, who was 26 when he won at California, his first Cup victory. Six winners last year were over 40, however, and five were 40 or older during this season's first 17 races.

"Obviously we've all been given great opportuni-

Jeff Gordon was just 22 when he won his first Winston Cup race. His success soon shifted the focus to younger drivers.

Harold Hinson

"It's always going to come back to who can win. The guy who's got five or 10 years, but not 20, under his belt and has got real talent and a good team is always going to be dominant."

—Max Muhleman,
motorsports marketing executive

"You're always going to have that confrontation between old and young, I guess, and it's a fine balance all the time just getting along with everybody."
—Kurt Busch

ties and great equipment," says Johnson. "A few of us have some great coaches to learn from, so we're all making the most of it. Don't be fooled. The veterans, they're on their game; they're up front battling and winning as well."

The driver leading the point race during much of the first half of the season was 45-year-old Sterling Marlin, a veteran in his 17th full season of competition. The point race by midseason produced an even mix of drivers in the top 10—five were over 40 and five were 31 or younger, including relative youngsters Gordon, Johnson, Stewart, Kenseth, and Busch.

Busch compares it to being a high school student, which he was just six years ago. "You're always going to have the elder statesmen and the younger statesmen," he says. "It's similar to high school where you've got freshmen coming in [and] they think they know everything; they're going to get on the varsity football team and do their own deal. Then, of course, you've got the veterans there who know how things are and they're going to put them in their place. You're always going to have that confrontation between old and young, I guess, and it's a fine balance all the time just getting along with everybody."

Muhleman sees the sport going through a normal transition and not a profound, landscape-altering trend toward younger drivers, as Marlin, Dale Jarrett, Rusty Wallace, Terry Labonte, and other over-40 drivers near the end of their careers.

"It's always going to come back to who can win," says Muhleman. "The guy who's got five or 10 years, but not 20, under his belt and has got real talent and a good team is always going to be dominant. They're going to win with all things being anywhere near equal.

"It's a cycle, really, that sometimes has not been as obvious as other times. Right now it's a very obvious thing. These guys are going to get old. In five years, they'll be five years older. I don't mean to be facetious, but Jeff Gordon is 30 and he's not included with the young guys anymore. I mean, it seems like yesterday [Dale] Earnhardt and everybody was calling him 'Wonder Boy,' and now, while he's not 'Pops' yet, he's not ever mentioned as a younger driver. Isn't that amazing?"

PEOPLE'S CHOICE AWARDS 2002: BIGGEST SURPRISE

Jimmie Johnson

From *Stock Car Racing*, November 2002

Jimmie Johnson proved his Daytona 500 pole award was no fluke. *Sam Sharpe*

Sure his car owner is Jeff Gordon, sure he's got the best equipment, but the 2002 season was supposed to be more of a learning curve for Jimmie Johnson. Instead, this guy goes out and quite often spanks most of the field. Go figure.

First of all, Johnson rolls out at Daytona and lands the pole for the 500. OK, just a fluke, right? After all, this former off-road racer hadn't exactly lit up the field in the NASCAR Busch Series, leaving with just one win.

But by the midseason of 2002, Johnson had reached Winston Cup's victory lane not once, but twice. He rested comfortably in third place in the point standings, a stone's throw from first and ahead of his boss. Hey Jimmie, didn't anyone ever tell you it's not cool to beat the boss?!

"Best rookie in memory," wrote Joseph G. Catuogno of Jupiter, Florida. Then again, it wasn't too awful long ago that Tony Stewart and Kevin Harvick were standing the racing world on its ear as a rookie. Now it's Johnson who may set the standard for how rookies will be judged in the future.

Johnson's confidence grows with each new race, and that's enough to keep even the wily veterans on edge. Some may argue that this fellow will only be another flash in the pan in racing history, but more likely we're witnessing the birth of the sport's next superstar.

Johnson climbed aboard for three wins in 2002.

Harold Hinson

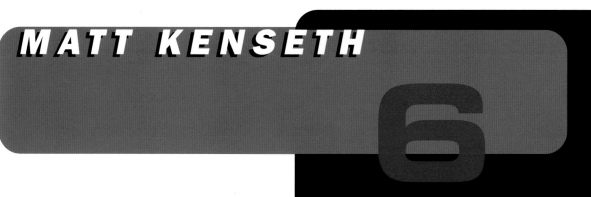

MATT KENSETH

Born: March 10, 1972

Hometown: Cambridge, Wisconsin

Height: 5-9

Weight: 150 lbs.

6

Sponsor	**Smirnoff Ice/ DeWalt Power Tools**
Make	**Ford**
Crew Chief	**Robbie Reiser**
Owner	**Mark Martin/Jack Roush**

NASCAR Winston Cup Career Statistics

Year	Races	Wins	Top 5s	Top 10s	Poles	Total Points	Final Standing	Winnings
1998	1	0	0	1	0	150	57	$42,340
1999	5	0	1	1	0	434	49	$143,561
2000	34	1	4	11	0	3,711	14	$2,408,138
2001	36	0	4	9	0	3,982	13	$2,565,579
2002	36	5	11	19	1	4,432	8	$3,766,347
Totals	112	6	20	41	1	12,709		$8,925,965

Matt Kenseth, now driving No. 17, got his opportunity to race in the Winston Cup unexpectedly. In September 1998, he filled in for Bill Elliott in the MBNA Gold 400 because Elliott was attending his father's funeral. *Nigel Kinrade*

WHO IS THIS GUY MATT KENSETH?

BY FR. DALE GRUBBA
From *Stock Car Racing*, July 1998

In 1993, Matt Kenseth was 21 and racing the local Wisconsin tracks. He's come a long way since then. *Fr. Dale Grubba*

"**I**f you don't feel like you are ready, we don't have to go to Talladega," Busch Series team owner Robbie Reiser told his rookie driver, Matt Kenseth. Perhaps Reiser was thinking of his own past experiences, one of which was a trip to the hospital in the back of an ambulance after an especially fearsome wreck at Talladega. Then, too, before Kenseth got the seat, Reiser had been mostly straightening bent race cars. "If you don't feel like you are ready . . ."

"No! No! I want to go!" declared the 24-year-old Kenseth, who had been making a name for himself on the short tracks.

Reiser, from Allentown, Wisconsin, and Kenseth had been together for just one week.

Kenseth started 1997 driving mainly in local events for Jerry Gunderman, whose other drivers had included Bobby Allison, Mark Martin, and Ted Musgrave. Kenseth qualified third and finished second at Kenly, North Carolina. The next weekend he crashed during a Hooters race at Rougemont, North Carolina, and was on his way home when Reiser called. Reiser's driver, Tim Bender, had been hurt in an accident and Reiser needed someone to take his place. Although Kenseth had driven just one race in the Busch Series,

Reiser offered him the job. Not long ago, both Reiser and Kenseth were Wisconsin-area drivers.

"Matt and I used to have some fierce races against each other," says Reiser. "I needed someone who understood race cars the way I understood them. I knew he could drive and he could talk to me in a manner I could understand."

Reiser told Kenseth, "You have to be at Nashville for the rookie meeting on Thursday. We have one car left. You have to make the race and finish it!"

Kenseth faced the decision of sticking with the cars he knew or moving up to the Busch Series full time. "Leaving Gunderman was hard," says Kenseth. "I had committed myself for a year. I know I let Jerry down, but this was a once-in-a-lifetime deal."

In his first run for Reiser and just his second-ever Busch Series start, Kenseth qualified third at Nashville and was running third when he spun in the final laps and finished 11th.

The next race on the schedule was Talladega.

"Except for the fall race at Charlotte in 1996, it was my first time in the draft," Kenseth remembers. "Before the first practice Robbie told me to be careful. Just go out and ride at the end of a train."

He sure figured it out in a hurry. Kenseth qualified 20th and moved forward 13 spots to finish 7th.

"There I was with Randy LaJoie, Michael Waltrip, Jeff Burton, and Mark Martin. I pulled out and Jeff Burton pushed me to the front. I kept going until Reiser came on the radio and told me that if I didn't come in I would run out of gas. It was the neatest feeling I have ever had in a race car.

"I feel more comfortable in the Busch car than I do in a late model. Drafting is tricky. It is like having a big tractor tire around the car. When you come up on a car, the tendency is to back off because you think you are going to hit it. You never touch. You push the car. There is a cushion of air around you."

Kenseth was impressive for the rest of the year. When the season ended, his score card showed a pair of top five finishes (thirds at Dover and California) and two races led.

On Saturday, February 22, 1998, at Rockingham, North Carolina, in his 24th start in the series, Matt Kenseth nudged his way by Tony Stewart on the final turn of the final lap for his first Busch Grand National victory. Afterward Mark Martin said that in his view Kenseth was the next big star. He said Jack Roush should sign him up.

Kenseth's progression from Wisconsin short tracks to the big league has been swift and event-filled. He started his career in 1988 while he was just a 16-year-old sophomore at Cambridge High School.

"My dad bought a car when I was 13 and raced it at Madison," Matt recalls. "Neither of us knew much and it was a learning experience. He continued to race in 1988 and 1989. My first car—what might be considered a sportsman—was a 1981 Camaro that Todd Kropf had driven to championships at Madison and Columbus. On the third night out I won a feature. I ran 15 features in 1988 and won two of them."

"The first night out in the Kropf car Matt won a heat race," says his dad, Roy Kenseth. "The third night he won the feature by holding off two of the best drivers at [the track], Pete Moore and Dave Phillips, for 20 laps. Matt was smooth. I knew then he was going to be a racer."

"In 1989 I bought a new car and ran at Wisconsin Dells for the points title," Matt continues. "Cub Resin, Dick Verdot, and some of the other drivers were tough competition, but I managed to finish second in points and win eight features. We also ran half a year at Columbus and a half year at Golden Sands plus some races at Slinger."

Kenseth's most memorable night in the 1989 campaign came at Slinger. He and late-model driver Ted Musgrave both arrived at the track with ill-handling cars. Both fixed their cars, both got fast time, and both won their respective features.

At the end of the season Matt's dad quit driving, demoralized that his son was faster than he was. "When I saw he could beat me, I quit. I had told him when he was 14, 'You work on the car. I'll drive. In the end you will know more than me.' "

In 1990 Kenseth bought a late model from Richie Bickle, who was making his own presence felt on the Wisconsin short tracks. "I ran Slinger. In the opening race I was following the leader, Tony Strupp. When he had a flat tire, I inherited the lead and won the race. I didn't win another feature the rest of the year, but I finished sixth in the points at Slinger and won the rookie-of-the-year title."

Kenseth also continued to broaden his experience by entering 15 ARTGO shows and running 40 features that summer.

The following summer, at age 19, Kenseth won at LaCrosse to become the youngest driver ever to win an ARTGO show, breaking Mark Martin's record. Kenseth did it by passing Joe Shear and Steve Holzhausen, then passing and holding off Steve and Tom Carlson.

The year 1992 was one that challenged Kenseth's desire. He won just three races and blew more engines

In 1995, Kenseth was winning ARTGO races. This victory photo was taken after a win at LaCrosse on July 12. *SCR Archives*

than he could count. By the end of the season, he was ready to quit.

"I felt we were at a standstill," he says. "I wasn't gaining. My dad and I had some major discussions at the end of the year. We had to find the dollars for a good program or I told him I would rather not race. It sounds silly. I was only 20 years old.

"Rick Kipley of Kipley Performance probably saved me by putting together a great motor program for us. He loaned us a motor for the final race of the season, the LaCrosse Oktoberfest, and we ran well.

"We built a new car from scratch for the 1993 season, installed a Kipley motor, and ran Madison. We won eight features and finished second in the points."

"We were the little guys on a big street in oval track racing," says Kipley. "We had been building motors for the national pulling circuit and wanted to expand. Roy and Matt were both focused and serious about what they were doing. Matt was a clean-cut guy who had his head on straight, both on and off the track."

Other opportunities presented themselves. Kenseth teamed up with Mike Butz, and though it was a struggle at first, eventually they won some races.

At the end of the season he and his dad campaigned their own car at Madison, where he won the final Short Track Series Race, LaCrosse, and Odessa, Missouri.

"It gave us a lot of confidence for 1994," Kenseth says. The 1994 and 1995 seasons established Kenseth as a short-track star. He ran 60 times in three different rides. Kenseth won track championships at both Madison (where he won 12 of 17 features) and Kaukauna.

Running for the same teams and a similar schedule in 1995, Kenseth successfully defended his titles at Madison and Kaukauna. He also won the Red, White, and Blue Series at Kaukauna.

"We knew by 1995 that Matt had too much talent to be with us for very long," says Patty Butz.

Mark Martin helped get Kenseth into a Roush Racing ride. *Fr. Dale Grubba*

She was right. In 1996 engine builder Carl Wegner got together with Kenseth, and together they went after a Hooters ProCup championship. Wegner liked Kenseth because he worked on his own cars and was quick to learn. He was more than a driver. With Paul Paoli and Paul Christman as crewmen, Kenseth moved to the Charlotte area to work out of Wegner's shop. The plan was to run the Hooters Series, five NASCAR truck races, five Busch races, and then in 1997 the whole Busch Series.

The team won one Hooters race and finished third in the points. They entered the spring race at Charlotte in a car Wegner rented from Bobby Dotter and finished 22nd after starting 30th.

The year was a disappointing one because they were unable to attract sponsorship. "I would just as soon forget it," Wegner says.

"It was like 1992," adds Kenseth. "Plans just didn't work. I thought things would be different. Personally, I had moved and was adjusting to being a thousand miles from home."

At the end of the summer the Wegner/Kenseth team dissolved and Matt went back to Wisconsin searching for another ride. He found one at Jerry Gunderman's shop, but two races into the 1997 season, a fateful call from Robbie Reiser changed everything.

Years ago another boy racer from Arkansas toured Wisconsin. His name was Mark Martin and it seemed that he stayed 18 years old forever. Matt Kenseth has many of the same qualities. "First impression?" says Patty Butz. "Quick witted . . . fast thinker . . . bubbly . . . very friendly . . . just a bit shy."

In some ways Matt's career mirrors Jeff Gordon's. Matt's father, Roy, began to shape his career when Matt was 14, just as Gordon's stepfather began to shape Gordon's career when Jeff was very young. Like Gordon, Kenseth stays in a racing division only long enough to gain the confidence and experience needed to move on to the next level. When he moves up, not much is expected, but he consistently delivers more than anyone might hope for.

After touring the neighbors' fields on a three-wheeler and mini-bike, a two-year run in the sportsman division, and some 60 wins in the late-model division, Matt Kenseth has arrived on the Busch Grand National scene hoping to move up to Winston Cup. It shouldn't be a surprise that Jack Roush has taken notice. Kenseth brings to the table the smoothness, focus, and talent seen in racing's champions.

Kenseth enters Slinger's victory lane in 1994 after winning the Wisconsin Short Track Series. *Fr. Dale Grubba*

THE NEXT BIG NAME IN STOCK CAR RACING

BY KERRY CRAMER
From *Stock Car Racing*, June 1999

This Busch Grand National Series Top Contender Is Ready to Make the Jump to Winston Cup

O pportunity often knocks when it's least expected. For Busch Grand National top contender Matt Kenseth, the opportunity to show the racing world that he could run Winston Cup came knocking on his door at Dover Downs Speedway in September 1998.

He was standing in the pits when Bill Elliott's crew chief approached him and offered to let him drive Elliott's car in the MBNA Gold 400. Elliott was attending his father's funeral, and the team needed a driver. Kenseth's

Winston Cup debut came unexpectedly. He met the challenge and emerged the hero of the day. He finished sixth, following, in order, Mark Martin, Jeff Gordon, Jeremy Mayfield, Bobby Labonte, and Rusty Wallace. Kenseth says he wasn't prepared for that race—who would be? But he finished near the top anyway.

He showed the world that he could be competitive and turned an already good relationship with Roush Racing and Mark Martin into a full-blown love affair. As of this writing in early March, plans were being laid to make Matt Kenseth the newest addition to the Roush Racing empire. The details of the deal are still in the works, but sources at Roush Racing say Roush will finance Kenseth's team. Kenseth will switch from Chevrolet to Ford, and Robbie Reiser will be the crew chief and owner. No sponsor has been announced. Jack Roush told *Stock Car Racing* he is considering the prospect of supporting Kenseth, and he doesn't know how he's going to do that yet. It's worth noting that current Winston Cup rules limit team sizes to two cars, and the other three cars in the Roush stable are owned by close family members. This car will probably still be owned by Robbie Reiser, yet financed by Roush. The details have yet to be determined, but the cogs are in motion to make it happen, according to Roush.

The 1999 Busch Team

Expectations are high for Matt Kenseth to have a championship season in the competitive 1999 Busch field. The 1998 points battle was a close one between him and BGN points champ Dale Earnhardt Jr. In the end, 48 points separated Earnhardt Jr. and BGN rookie Kenseth. Look for the battle to continue in 1999.

"We learned what it was like to race and be competitive," Kenseth says of the 1998 season. If 1998 was a learning season, and he finished in second place, logically one can expect even better performances as seat time increases and he becomes more familiar with tracks.

DeWalt High Performance Tools replaced Lycos as the primary sponsor on the No. 17 Chevrolet Monte

Matt Kenseth's success in the Busch Series turned heads. *Nigel Kinrade*

Carlo team owned by Reiser, who is also crew chief for the team. Kenseth says DeWalt is an awesome sponsor because it's a young company, and he's a young guy—just 27 years old. DeWalt has been building heavy-duty tools since 1992.

A Strong Racing History

Matt Kenseth grew up in Cambridge, Wisconsin. He developed a strong interest in racing around the age of 13 at the Jefferson Speedway in Jefferson, Wisconsin. Things started to happen for him in 1994 when he captured track titles at Wisconsin International Raceway and Madison International Speedway. He broke a record that still stands for the most feature wins at Madison, with 12. That year also gave him the title as the youngest driver ever to win the Miller Genuine Draft National championships.

The wins continued in 1995 as he scored four consecutive feature wins at Kaukauna. In 1996, he finished third in the Hooters Series and made his Busch Series debut at Charlotte. He competed in the ASA series in 1997 and was second in points before moving to Reiser Enterprises to do BGN full time. The 1998 season marks Kenseth's first full BGN schedule and his Winston Cup debut at Dover, where he drove Bill Elliott's No. 94 McDonald's Ford. Overall, his second-place BGN points finish netted $798,000 in winnings during the course of the year.

This year brings new sponsorship for Kenseth (he was unpacking a box of DeWalt tools as we interviewed him, referring to the company as "awesome") and the prospect of moving up to Winston Cup with the support of Roush Racing is on his doorstep. He says he feels lucky to be placed with a team that works so hard. He often receives advice from Mark Martin, who helped him hook up with Roush. He gets along well with his crew chief and car owner Robbie Reiser, whom he used to race against in Wisconsin.

Much of his driving style isn't by design, he admits. It's aggressive when the situation calls for it, but he mainly focuses on saving as much of the car as possible for the end of the race.

Kenseth made waves in 1998 in the Busch Grand National Division, placing second in overall points with three victories, 17 top 5 finishes, and 23 top 10 finishes.

Shocking Revelations

Kenseth doesn't really do much hands-on stuff to his cars, but he does have one technical passion.

That is shock science. Since BGN teams don't have shock guys like the Winston Cup teams, he has taken it upon himself to learn the ins and outs of this important facet of chassis-tuning. He spends extra time with a shock dyno and says he sticks to the basics, and the results of his labor show up at the track.

One of the most important aspects of his current team, he says, is the individual team members. His attitude is that nobody is more important than anybody else on the team. They all have to pull their own weight because even just one guy can mess up a team. His recipe for success is being with a good race team and surrounding himself with good people and good equipment. His advice for aspiring drivers is not to get stuck in a rut at one track. He tells them to go around to different ones and get noticed. And above all else, win races at whatever you do—whether it's Sportsman, late model, or anything with wheels.

Current Events

Kenseth won his first Busch Series race in last year's spring race at Rockingham. The Reiser Enterprises team went to Rockingham last February unsponsored and unsure if it would be able to run the entire Busch Series schedule. The team went on to capture two more wins in 1998 and finished second in the championship points battle. Last year he captured the most top 5s and top 10s of any driver in the series, taking 17 top 5s and 23 top 10s. For the sake of comparison, Dale Earnhardt Jr. had 16 top 5s, 22 top 10s, and seven wins. Kenseth had three wins in 1998. For those who don't want to get out a calculator to figure out the previous sentences, Kenseth showed he was capable of being consistently good.

He started the 1999 season in Daytona with a fourth-place finish. In Rockingham he finished third. Kenseth has a love-hate relationship with Rockingham. "It's cool to go back there," says Kenseth. "Rockingham has been weird to us; we've run really good there one time and really bad there two other times. I have only run the spring race at Rockingham once, and we were able to win that race." Last year his car was unsponsored in victory lane. Showing up in victory lane solved that problem when Lycos came on board as a primary sponsor.

Although nothing is set in stone and nobody has signed on the dotted line with Roush yet, Kenseth's future at Roush should be a natural fit. The opportunity to be one of the best is right on his doorstep. And when it's Jack Roush knocking, talented race drivers are quick to open the door.

TONY STEWART, DALE EARNHARDT JR., AND MATT KENSETH

BY BOB MYERS
From *Circle Track*, October 1999

Three of NASCAR's Hottest Rising Stars

Running tight—Earnhardt Jr. (8) puts the pressure on Kenseth (17). *Nigel Kinrade*

et's return to Lowe's Motor Speedway near Charlotte in May and rejoin Tony Stewart, Dale Earnhardt Jr., and Matt Kenseth, twentysomethings who seem destined to be faces and forces in NASCAR Winston Cup's near future.

The blue-chip drivers, yearlings all in terms of Winston Cup, have competed in several races since May, but at Lowe's indelible memories were cast for a lifetime. Stewart, 28, demonstrated that he's probably the best first-year Winston Cup driver since Jeff Gordon. Defending Busch Series Champion Earnhardt Jr., 24, made his long-awaited and ballyhooed major-league debut impressively, and Busch star Kenseth, 27, got a multiyear, big-league contract from Jack Roush and Mark Martin.

Matt Kenseth: Moving On Up

No driver is more excited about the future than Kenseth, not even Stewart and Little E. In about 15 months, Kenseth has vaulted from obscurity into the limelight. He had scored six Busch victories through the 300 at Lowe's, including his first at Rockingham early last season. At the time, Reiser Racing, owned and led by Robbie Reiser, was small and modestly sponsored. Kenseth finished second to Little E in points last year and was leading the standings after 14 races this season.

Roush and Martin were watching. Now Kenseth has behind him the vast resources of Roush Racing, Winston Cup's largest organization; the support of DeWalt tools; and the experience and knowledge of superstar Martin, a partner with Roush in the team. He is to run five Winston Cup races this season in the No. 17 (the number is courtesy of Darrell Waltrip) Roush Ford, including the fall events at Darlington, Dover, Charlotte, and Rockingham, leading to the full schedule in 2000.

"We have been watching the Kenseth-Reiser combination with a great deal of interest over the past two years," says Roush. "Their progression through the Busch Series has been remarkable in some sense. Matt has shown extraordinary maturity and patience for a relatively young driver and has demonstrated, with Robbie, that he knows the mechanics of his race cars. We expect this combination will produce a championship-level effort for many years." If Kenseth's impressive sixth place in Bill Elliott's Ford in his only pre-Roush Winston Cup outing, at Dover last year, is a criterion, he's a keeper.

"It's a dream come true," says Kenseth, a Cambridge, Wisconsin, native. "A few years ago, I didn't think I'd ever get into NASCAR."

The month of May had a happy ending for three youngsters with dreams, and when you look at the progress and resources for each one, the future looks bright. It's hard to imagine that these men won't soon be slugging it out on the track for a Winston Cup championship berth.

OVERSHADOWED NO LONGER

BY BOB MYERS
From *Circle Track*, November 2000

Matt Kenseth is the other guy.

For more than two years, Kenseth has been racing in the shadow of the competitor and friend with the famous name—Dale Earnhardt Jr.

In terms of attention and deeds, Kenseth has trailed by a few car lengths, so to speak. At almost every turn, the blue-blood son of Dale Earnhardt seems to get there first. Kenseth finished second and third to NASCAR's latest phenom and won six fewer races in his battles with the champion for the past two Busch Series championships.

In their rookie year in Winston Cup, Kenseth spotted Junior three victories, including the nonpoints The Winston All-star Classic, before he nailed his own first triumph in the prestigious Coca-Cola 600 at

Charlotte. Junior won in his 12th Winston Cup start, at Texas Motor Speedway, Kenseth in his 18th.

Now the runaway leaders of the freshman class are engaged in another exciting battle, this time for Raybestos Rookie of the Year honors, and it appears that once again, the battle will go down to the wire.

Kenseth, a native of Cambridge, Wisconsin, a small town 20 minutes from Madison, was still anonymous in NASCAR circles when he came to the Busch Series in 1997. He is not surprised that Little Earnhardt is a media darling or that he is living up to his heritage. He is neither envious nor bothered.

"Dale Jr. gets a little more coverage than I do, and he is flashier than I am," says Kenseth, "but he deserves everything he gets. He doesn't have success because his name is Earnhardt. He's earned it. I am sure that his name helped him in the beginning, but his performances behind the wheel got him where he is. He's an awesome driver, very talented. He has won more races and championships than I have. I have a lot of respect for what he has done. I knew the media would be focused on him, but that's all right with me. Maybe he's taken some of the heat off me. Right now, we're getting plenty of attention."

Fast Friends

Kenseth, 28, and Little E, 25, first met by accident. Junior drove into the side of Kenseth's car during a Busch race and wanted to say he was sorry. It was no big deal, Kenseth told him. They admire, respect, and support each other. At the track, their motor coaches are parked alongside each other, and they hang out and talk racing. The rivalry, other than the natural aspect of Junior driving a Chevrolet and Kenseth a Ford, is largely media-driven. When Little E got his first Winston Cup victory, Kenseth, who had crashed out and was heartbroken because he had been in position to win, was unable to join in the cele-

It didn't take long after entering Winston Cup racing before Kenseth became one of the sport's up-and-upcoming drivers. *Nigel Kinradd*

Because he had raced Kenseth in Wisconsin, Robbie Reiser (left) knew he had a real racer when he hired Kenseth to drive his Busch car. Now Reiser is Kenseth's crew chief in the Winston Cup series. *Nigel Kinrade*

bration. But he left a note of congratulations under the door of Junior's motor coach. "He thought that was cool," says Kenseth, using a favorite expression.

Junior joined Kenseth in the winner's circle at Charlotte. "That meant a lot to me," says Kenseth, "especially after a race that he had dominated until the final pit stop and was disappointed not to win. It made me feel really good, and it showed a lot of maturity on his part. I think he felt a little uncomfortable about being there too long, that he was stealing the spotlight, but that wasn't the case at all.

"We get along well, but we don't do much away from the track," Kenseth explains about his relationship with Junior. "We're different—our lifestyles are different at this stage. He has some kid left in him and is in the wild and have-fun stage. That's the way I was five years ago. I'm quiet and reserved—until you get to know me, then I have my obnoxious moments. I'm three years older. I don't know if I'm more mature, but I'm more settled."

A Good Choice of Role Models

Mark Martin, one of Winston Cup's superstar drivers, was in the winner's circle for the first time as a car owner when Kenseth won at Charlotte. Martin is Kenseth's mentor and co-owns the No. 17 team with multiteam magnate Jack Roush. They brought Kenseth and his crew chief, Robbie Reiser, to Winston Cup as part of Roush Racing. Reiser, a former driver and Kenseth archrival when the two raced the bullrings of Wisconsin, gave the young driver his break into the Busch Series and has been with him ever since. Kenseth is the lucky rookie because he has the knowledge and abundant resources of Martin, Roush Racing, and primary sponsor DeWalt Tools behind him.

"Matt is doing great," says Martin. "He's already won and finished second. It's not like he is a rookie. He has lots of experience for his age. He hasn't gotten in the way and hasn't caused any problems. He's a sponsor's dream and gets along great with the media. He could be awfully good—a big winner."

"I thought Mark was about as happy for me as he could be when I won my first Busch race with Robbie at Rockingham in 1998," Kenseth says. "We didn't have a sponsor on the car at the time and were hurting for money. Mark and Roush Racing took care of that quickly. But I think Mark was even happier at Charlotte."

In the first 15 Winston Cup races this season, Kenseth logged a win, three top 5s, five top 10s, and was ranked 11th in championship points (Junior was 14th). Only four times did he finish 21st or lower, and he held a slight lead over Earnhardt Jr. in the rookie competition.

Having already exceeded some goals, Kenseth says a top 10 finish in championship points is realistic. To do that, he says he will have to improve at the tracks that are difficult for him, experience few mechanical failures, and keep the team on the same page.

"I have a lot easier time getting around a banked track than I do a flat track," Kenseth says. "I dislike places like Martinsville and New Hampshire because they're flat. I love Dover's banks. I am not a good road racer at all."

Of course, Kenseth wants to be rookie of the year, but that's not his primary objective. "The main focus is to be a contender every weekend, whether it's this year or next," he says, "to run in the top five and establish consistency."

One of Kenseth's strengths is that he is tireless in working with his crew to make his Fords as fast as possible. *Sam Sharpe*

Reiser, who counts 20 Winston Cup rookies among his 25-member race team, adds, "I'd like to see us a strong contender in the last five races this year—and compete for the championship next year."

Reiser, also a Wisconsin native, is high on Kenseth and echoes Martin's praises. "He is a good driver with a lot of racing intelligence and savvy," he says. "He's very heads-up and a team player. His strength is the ability to feel a race car and know what to change. He never gives up on anything. He works until he runs out of time, trying to make his car the way he wants it. Obviously, we can't get it right 35 times a year, so he sucks it up and drives what we give him."

No Flash, Just Fast

Kenseth's style is more conservative than Earnhardt Jr.'s or Tony Stewart's, the two drivers with whom he is often compared. Kenseth's demeanor on the track is more like Terry Labonte's. Sometimes he seems to appear at the front as if from out of nowhere.

"I try to take care of my car and tires and be up front when it counts," he says. "I want the car to stay consistent. I'd rather be slower at the start and faster at the end. If I could qualify better, maybe I'd be up front all the time."

Kenseth is a midpack qualifier, missing the top 25 five times and compiling an average starting position of 22.5 in the first 15 races. "Matt doesn't push himself over his limit in qualifying," says Reiser. "He won't try to get away with a lap over his head. Qualifying is a team weakness we need to work on. It's not altogether Matt."

Kenseth thinks enough of Reiser that when he signed with Martin and Roush to drive in Winston Cup, he made sure Reiser was included in the deal, "because he's the one who got me involved in the Busch Series," Kenseth says. "We get along and communicate very well. He's doing a good job getting everything organized and covering the bases."

The union between Kenseth and Reiser is unique because they are former adversaries—fierce rivals when they raced against each other in late models on Wisconsin's short tracks from 1990 to 1993. "I won't say we were enemies, but we certainly weren't friends," recalls Reiser. "I am six years older [34] than Matt and had more experience. He was the new kid on the scene. We both raced for a living, and I felt he was there to take my grocery money. I won 11 championships, but everything I won in late models, it seemed he was second or third."

In 1994 Reiser left Wisconsin to establish a Busch team. He bought land and a couple of used cars and built a shop in Denver, North Carolina. A year later he ran out of money, parked his cars, and began installing piers at lakefront homes for a living. Racers Ricky Rudd, Jimmy Spencer, and Buddy Parrott were among his clients. Eventually, Reiser struck a deal with Kraft Foods to put driver Tim Bender in his Busch cars. Unfortunately, Bender was injured in just the eighth race of the 1997 season. Reiser had to find a driver in two days.

"I wanted to drive myself, but I knew I had to run the business," says Reiser. "The only driver I could think

of with potential was Matt Kenseth. I hired Matt even though Kraft made it clear I'd lose the sponsorship at the end of the season because he was a rookie."

By this time Kenseth had won a bunch of races and short-track championships, raced in NASCAR's All-Pro and Hooters ProCup series, and landed a top ride in the American Speed Association (ASA) with successful owner Jerry Gunderman, whose driving alumni include Martin, Ted Musgrave, and the late Alan Kulwicki. "I didn't know what to expect with Robbie," Kenseth says, "but I had not received any other opportunities to drive in the Busch Series. It seemed like a chance to show what I could do."

It was. Kenseth finished 11th in his debut at Nashville and 6th at Talladega. In 21 starts, Kenseth had two top 5s, seven top 10s, and was second to Steve Park as the top rookie. While at Talladega, Kenseth met Martin, which led to his second big break.

"Of course I knew of Mark, but I hadn't met him," says Kenseth. "During the drivers' meeting at Talladega, he introduced himself. The next week, he called and told me he and Roush Racing wanted to help me with my career and pave my way to Winston Cup. I was surprised and flattered. I was excited, but at the same time, Mark had a lot of high hopes and expectations on what we might accomplish, and I didn't have any idea we would have a chance to do that. At the time, I didn't even have a top five in Busch, and I didn't know why he was interested in me. I'm sure glad he was."

"I am a race fan and keep up with what goes on in other racing circles," Martin explains. "I was aware of this kid in Wisconsin winning a lot of races in different kinds of stock cars. That told me he wasn't relying on a crew chief to make his cars go fast—that he had a lot of mechanical knowledge. That's my kind of guy. Once we met, I was very impressed with him. He's a guy who is easy to help. I wanted to see him

Kenseth's career got a big boost when Mark Martin decided to take the young driver under his wing. Martin even helped Kenseth land a Winston Cup ride with Roush Racing.

Jeff Huneycutt

reach his full potential. I like helping people and want to do more of that in the future.

"On top of that, I have driven for and been devoted to Roush Racing for about 13 years. I felt that if I didn't act quickly, we wouldn't have a shot at Matt. Getting him is really paying off."

Kenseth continues to drive a limited Busch schedule—races that do not conflict with Winston Cup—this season for Reiser's team, which Reiser's father, John, oversees. That has provided an opportunity for Jason Schuler, 28, a high school classmate of Kenseth, to drive the No. 17 Visine Chevrolet when Kenseth isn't able to man the controls. Kenseth won twice and had eight top 5s in his first 12 Busch outings this season.

Kenseth, who plans to marry his fiancée in December, is happy with racing and his life. He says it's a blessing ("It's cool.") to be driving for Martin and Roush Racing as a rookie.

"I have been fortunate most of my career to have good equipment, to be with good people, and to run up front," he says. "I think there are a lot of people who would like to be in my shoes."

Perhaps, but it takes a lot more than just shoes to be a class act and a winning driver.

Kenseth wasn't the only rookie on the No. 17 team in 2002. Most of his crew graduated from the Busch Series to support Kenseth's effort in Winston Cup. *Sam Sharpe*

Kenseth, who got his big break into the Busch Series thanks to former rival Robbie Reiser (right), showed his loyalty when he insisted Reiser join him as crew chief on his Winston Cup team with Roush Racing. *Rusty Huband*

SOPHOMORE BLUES

BY MATT KENSETH
From *Stock Car Racing*, January 2002

Kenseth faced tough times in 2001, the season after his rookie-of-the-year campaign.

Nigel Kinrade

Man, I cannot wait to see 2002 come. To say the 2001 season was tough is an understatement.

At the beginning of 2001, everyone was asking me about the sophomore jinx. I never thought twice about it, and I sure never thought it would happen to us. Even though I am not superstitious, what happened to us last year could very well be classified as the jinx. Just like Murphy's Law, everything that could go wrong—on the track—did.

We went into last season with high expectations. Of course our fans, the media and my fellow competitors also had certain expectations of the DeWalt team as well. I can tell you one thing: Because we did not live up to all of the expectations, no one was harder on us than we were on ourselves.

On the other hand, we do have the potential to become a championship caliber team, and there were a few races this past year in which we had the car to beat. For some reason, winning races just was not in the cards for us in 2001. It seemed like there were always circumstances, either beyond my control or unavoidable accidents, preventing us from good finishes. The best example of this was the second race in Michigan. Even Mother Nature dealt us a bad hand. If the race had gone until the end, I would have pulled into victory lane. But instead, we settled for fourth.

All year long, people asked what our problem was. My answer was, "If we could just put our finger on it, we would fix it." Looking back now, I think the main problem was qualifying. If you qualify in the back every week, you are going to get caught up in someone else's mistake. By starting in the back, we were forced to fight our way to the front. I depended on my team to help me get to the front with good pit stops and strategy. They depended on me to drive the heck out of the race car.

When you have an awful season like we did, it makes you look at the bigger picture. There were so many significant events that changed the sport and the world, it just made the little things look totally minute. Just to name a few, starting off the year losing another competitor and friend, Dale Earnhardt, cast a dark cloud over NASCAR for the whole season. Imagine what Dale Jr. went through this year, trying to work through the grieving process of losing his dad and yet focus on racing. It was amazing to watch, and we were so happy to see him win the Pepsi 400 because he raced hard, and he deserved it.

Also, witnessing the terrorist attacks on New York and Washington, D.C., where the loss of life

was so tremendous. NASCAR cancelled the race in New Hampshire that weekend out of respect for the country, which was a good decision. It's still hard to talk about it. I think it was just a shock to everyone. Our hearts still go out to those families who lost loved ones.

In my personal life, last year could not have gone better. Katie and I enjoyed our first year as husband and wife. I am so thankful for Katie, my parents and my son, Ross. They are always there for me when things get tough, and they helped me keep my chin up through a terrible season.

The year 2002 is a brand-new season, and I am looking forward to it. NASCAR has been taking us into brand-new markets, and the sport is getting bigger and better every day. I never thought when I was a kid growing up in Wisconsin I would be a part of the elite Winston Cup Series. I think I have come

a long way since the days when I rigged my dad's riding lawnmower to go faster and rode it through the streets of Cambridge, Wisconsin. My dad nicknamed me "Motor" because while other kids my age were out riding bikes and playing sports, I was busy tinkering with anything that had a motor in it. Even as I look back now, it makes me laugh, but it also makes me appreciate the support of my family and how we all worked hard to make my dreams of racing a reality.

My crew chief Robbie Reiser and my team have really worked hard on pit stops, on the motor program and in the body shop. Look for the DeWalt car to be up front a lot more in 2002 because one bad season is behind us, and we don't plan on having another one any time soon. This experience has made us stronger and like the slogan for my sponsor DeWalt Tools says—"Guaranteed Tough."

Despite no wins, Kenseth salvaged a 13th-place finish in points in 2001. *Nigel Kinrade*

KENSETH ON THE ROUSH RESURGENCE

BY LARRY COTHREN
From *Stock Car Racing*, September 2002

The resurgence of Roush Racing this season has been led by Matt Kenseth, who started the year by winning two of the first seven Winston Cup races. After Kenseth finished 13th in points and posted no wins last season, he and teammates Mark Martin, Jeff Burton, and Kurt Busch are back at the front of the pack. Kenseth recently spoke to *Stock Car Racing* about the improvement.

Kenseth reversed his fortunes with a win at Rockingham in the second race of 2002.

Jesse Miles Jr.

"When your car is handling good and you can run up front and you can pass cars and you catch them and try to figure out how to get around them, that's when it's fun."

—Matt Kenseth

Your performance has improved dramatically this season. Was there a point last season when you began to doubt yourself?

I never really doubted I could drive the cars when they got them right. I just doubted my ability to figure out what was wrong with our cars because we were running so bad, and we were so far off that I couldn't tell them what to put in the car to make it better. That part I doubted. Our team morale, considering how bad we ran, stayed pretty good. Morale is going to get down when you run bad and there's absolutely nothing you can do about it. If I'm smiling at the shop and at the racetrack, I'll go home when I'm running bad and be miserable. It's tough to keep your chin up.

Stories circulated last year that you wanted out of Roush Racing. Was there any shopping around on your part or did other teams contact you?

Not really. You're always going to have people in the garage mention that "if something happens to your deal then call me," or something like that. It was never really anything more than that. Jack's been good to us as far as giving us the equipment that we need or the cars we want to build. I've still got some time left on my contract, and I never really considered last year doing anything different.

Is this the last year of your contract?

I've still got another year left.

Are you content at Roush Racing or do you plan to see what else is out there when your contract is up?

Right now we are running great and trying to contend for a championship. I am not going to worry about contracts or rumors in the middle of the racing season. I am going to concentrate on winning races and staying up in the point standings.

Were you surprised by the overall performance of Roush Racing last year?

Yeah, because when I came here in 1999 and ran my five-race deal, we ran really well in the five races. We didn't finish great in all of them but we ran pretty well, and it really wasn't much harder than the Busch Series for us to run well right away. I was feeling good about life. Mark, in 1998, won seven races and was second in points. Burton won a few races. Everything looked good. Everything looked like it was going to be great, and my rookie year started out really strong, started out really, really good. In the middle of my rookie year, we started a downhill slide and it just continued last year until the first of this season when it started coming back uphill, and it's still going up now.

How much has the one-engine rule for qualifying and racing helped Roush Racing this year?

We never put a lot of emphasis on qualifying engines. Instead of buying special parts and doing special stuff, we just pretty much used old race motors. Up till a few years ago, that would work just fine. But last year it was really getting out of control with people building qualifying motors. They would build a qualifying motor that was 40 to 50 more horsepower than their race motor. For me it was really tough qualifying. I felt like we were at a big deficit there. Even though you wouldn't know it from my average starting position this year, I think it's helped our qualifying quite a bit. Even for the race, we've always worked hard on race motors and our stuff is as durable, or more durable than most teams, and we haven't really had to detune our stuff. We've been able to keep improving our power where some people might have had to back their stuff up a little bit to run through an entire weekend.

You and crew chief Robbie Reiser go back to your ASA days when you drove against each other. How much does it mean to have him calling the shots?

It means a lot. We've worked together for a long time, since 1997. He's been pretty much my only crew chief [in NASCAR]. It's been great working with him. We understand what each other is saying. We don't always agree with what we're saying to each other, but we understand. We have a lot of trust in

each other. If I tell him I need something done on the car, need a setup that I just have to have, I know that I'm going to get it. We have a great relationship on the track and away from the track, too, so it makes it a lot more enjoyable.

If you look at Dale Earnhardt Jr. and consider that you guys came into Winston Cup together, and you've essentially equaled his success, does it bother you to see all the publicity he gets?

I would say the first couple of years I raced the Busch Series against him, he did run a little better than me and he won two championships. We were pretty strong, but he probably got 10 times the amount of publicity, and that was true even in our [Winston Cup] rookie year. It maybe irritated me a little inside, but I'll tell you a story. After Darlington this year he needed a ride home and asked to ride with me. My wife, Katie, and I were driving one of Jack's [Roush] Mustangs down there so we gave him a ride home.

We stopped at Wendy's to get a bite to eat and went inside to use the bathroom and then get food to go. Everybody in there recognized him and started screaming like we were at a rock concert and they had spotted a rock star. Little girls in there were screaming and cornered him and swarmed all around him. Nobody even noticed me. I didn't envy him one iota. If it was like that for me every day, it would drive me crazy. It really doesn't bother me at all anymore since that day. I enjoy my time away, and I enjoy being

The Rockingham win gave the DeWalt crew reason to celebrate, something they lacked in 2001. *Sam Sharpe* able to go where I want without necessarily being cornered all the time.

You ran several different series coming up—ASA, Hooters ProCup, NASCAR All-Pro, to name a few. What circuit would you recommend to a young driver attempting to move up?

That's a tough thing. If you look around in the Busch Series, in Winston Cup, everybody has his different route. There's not really a planned route. There's not an A, B, C, D, E, F route, where you start in A and then move on to B. A lot of it is luck, being recognized by the right person. The main thing I was lucky enough to do a lot, and I would suggest, would be to race as many different tracks as you can. Don't get stuck racing at the same track every week. I think it's really important to get out and race as many different types of racetracks as you can.

You have maturity about you that some of the younger drivers seem to lack. Does that come from your upbringing?

My dad, when he used to race, would get pretty hyper, and I used to get really hyper when I was younger and started racing. I would fly off the handle and stuff like that. There are some people who have taught me to keep my cool a little bit better, even though no one keeps it all the time. I really try to keep everything in perspective. When things go wrong, they go wrong; there's not really anything you can do about it. You need to take the highs and the lows. Last year we had a lot of lows so that was definitely a humbling experience. It makes you appreciate the highs a lot more.

How much more intense is the action on the track this year compared to your first two years in Winston Cup?

This sounds dumb but, to tell you the truth, the most intense racing that I've done was probably last year running in the back. Running in the back is really, really hard. When you're back there fighting for 20th and your car is handling terrible and you're fighting your car like crazy and you're trying to pass cars and get the best finish you can, it's really tough. When your car is handling good and you can run up front and you can pass cars and you catch them and try to figure out how to get around them, that's when it's fun. That's when it's maybe not as difficult, but it's difficult when your car is not handling good and you don't have the equipment underneath you to do as good as you think you can do and you're overdriving all the time to try to make the car go faster. That's the most intense racing you'll do. The most intense racing happens from about 19th to 27th.

What do you like least about the sport today?

The thing I like the least is how many rules there are and how they [NASCAR] take a lot of it out of the teams' hands. When I started racing, I really enjoyed trying to figure something out before the next guy. The things that bother me most is like the top five cars after a race they'll take the shocks apart and show everybody, even though there's no rule in what you can run in the shocks. They'll make an announcement in the garage and say, "OK, here's the shock teardown from last week," and they'll show everybody the shocks that you ran, and that's one of your only tuning tools left. Stuff like that frustrates me more than anything. There's just so many rules on so many things that they

Kenseth, shown with Jeff Gordon (right), possesses a cool demeanor that mirrors his maturity.

Sam Sharpe

don't leave you a lot of room to figure out stuff for yourself, so that part is really frustrating.

It's well known that Mark Martin has been a mentor of yours. Other than Mark, what veteran driver do you look up to?

There's a lot of them. Dale Jarrett is one of them and probably for a different reason. I remember when I was a little kid watching when he drove that Hardee's car and he ran really bad. It seems like he was always running in the back and having problems and was really struggling. Then to be able to come back and win races and be a Winston Cup champion, I think that is really cool. That says a lot about not giving up and keeping after it. To see somebody do that well after struggling early in their career, to me that is something that's really cool.

What do you do to relax in your spare time?

I just like to hang out. My wife and I built a little log cabin up in Wisconsin. My best friend from high school has some land out there also. When we get enough time off, I like to go up there and hang out for a few days. It's out in the middle of nowhere. There are no people around, and it's fun to get away and relax. No cities. No nothing. I like to do that.

Do you see your nine-year-old son, Ross, as much as you would like?

No, I don't get to see him near as much as I would like. He lives up in Wisconsin. I do get to see him, though, and he gets to come to some races. When I do get to spend some time with him, I enjoy that.

Is he a future racer?

Yeah, he's been racing some go karts and doing stuff like that. To be honest, I wish he wasn't, but he is though. I wish he was just playing football and baseball until he is at least a little bit older. I think he's a little too young.

A relationship built on trust helps Kenseth and crew chief Robbie Reiser (left) put the No. 17 DeWalt Ford at the front. *Harold Hinson*

Kenseth says the most intense racing on the track occurs from "about 19th to 27th."

Jeff Huneycutt

JAMIE McMURRAY

7

Born: June 3, 1976

Hometown: Joplin, Missouri

Height: 5-8

Weight: 150 lbs.

Sponsor	**Havoline**
Make	**Dodge**
Crew Chief	**Donnie Wingo**
Owner	**Chip Ganassi**

NASCAR Winston Cup Career Statistics

Year	Races	Wins	Top 5s	Top 10s	Poles	Total Points	Final Standing	Winnings
2002	6	1	1	2	0	679	46	$669,097

Jamie McMurray's win at Charlotte helped the team shake off the loss of regular driver Sterling Marlin to injury. *Harold Hinson*

McMURRAY ON
LIVING THE DREAM

BY LARRY COTHREN
From *Stock Car Racing*, February 2003

He dreamed of being a Winston Cup driver, but not in his wildest fantasies did Jamie McMurray expect to find himself in victory lane during the 2002 season. He's been pinched enough to know the win was real; now he speaks with *Stock Car Racing* about the reality check that will come when he moves to the series full time in 2003.

A jubilant McMurray celebrated his first Winston Cup win in just his second start. *Jesse Miles Jr.*

"You know, everything happens for a reason. ... I don't know what I've done to deserve this opportunity, but I feel really blessed and I'm trying to make the most of it."

—Jamie McMurray

Talk about everything that happened to you in the latter part of 2002, getting the Winston Cup offer from Chip Ganassi and winning at Lowe's Motor Speedway while subbing for Sterling Marlin.

It's all happened so fast. I didn't really know what I was going to do next season. I really wanted to stay with my Busch team. I told them I was going to as long as a great opportunity didn't come along to move on to Cup. When Chip contacted me about doing that for 2003, I couldn't imagine a better opportunity coming along in Winston Cup. I feel like they have just about the best organization there is. So I made the decision to move up and was really excited and trying to get prepared for that. Then when Sterling got hurt and they told me I was going to fill in for him the rest of the season, I knew that was a tough situation to step into, but it was going to be a good opportunity for me. At the same time, it could work both ways. If I had gotten into that and done well, it was going to be great for next season. If I had gotten in it and not

done well, it would have been a tough winter for me, for the team, and also for the sponsor.

Take us through the last laps of the win at Charlotte. What were you saying to your crew?

I had joked around with Lee [McCall, crew chief] and Tony [Glover, team manager] and all the guys throughout the whole race, trying to make jokes, and they were doing the same thing with me. But about the last 60 laps, I didn't say anything on the radio. I think the only thing I said was after my last green flag stop, about 10 laps into that, when I said my car was really starting to get good. Tire pressure was really building up. They were pretty much just saying, "Hit your marks. Stay focused." They were counting laps down and just cheering me on, building my confidence up. I didn't say anything until the last lap down the backstretch. I just started screaming; I was real excited. It's a feeling I'll never forget. It was more exciting two weeks later than it was at the time. At the time, I couldn't take it all in. Later I realized what we did. You read all the stuff on the Internet and all the letters that people sent congratulating me, and it was incredible, just the response I got.

That was one helluva burnout after the win. Had you been practicing?

No. I had never done a burnout before. I told my family and my girlfriend and everybody, when I get to do a burnout I'm going to do a great one. That was fourth gear as fast as it would go. That was tached out in fourth gear. That was cool. To be able to get in the car at a racetrack that I didn't care for and be able to go out and win was amazing.

In 1997 you were track champion at I-44 Speedway in Lebanon, Missouri. Did you dream that five years later you would be in victory lane for a Winston Cup race?

From 1994 to '97 or '98, I ran just local stock

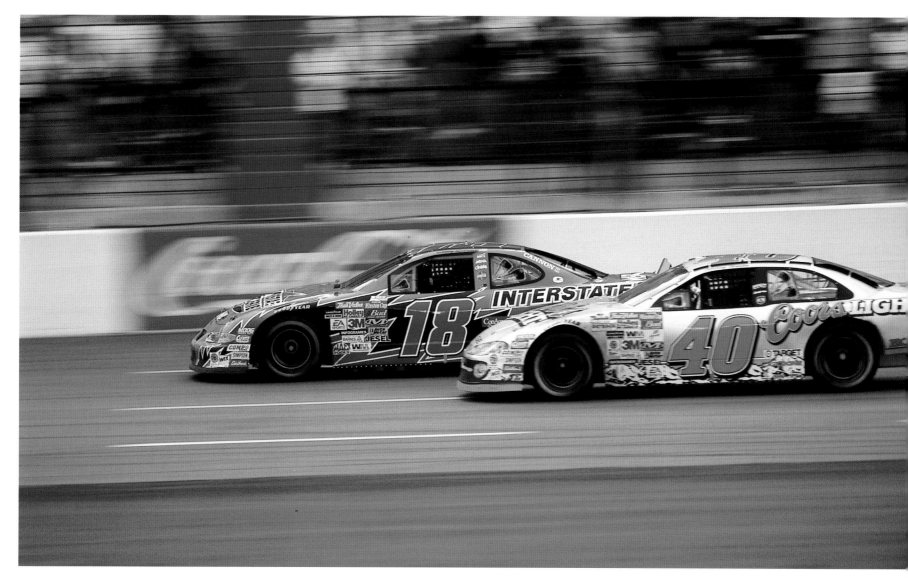

cars. Actually, before I started racing stock cars, I thought by the time I was 20 or 21 I would be in Winston Cup. I was not being realistic, just thinking that a national champion in go karts ought to move up. I ran stock cars for two, three, four years, and in '98 I remember thinking, "What do you have to do to move up?" Everybody was telling us, "Oh, bring money and you can drive our car." I thought, "God, how is it ever going to happen?" Then I got an opportunity from Mike Mitler in 1999 to go run five truck races in his truck. At the end of '99 I moved to St. Louis where his shop was, and he gave me a job. We set out to go run as many truck races as we could in 2000. Halfway through the year 2000, I got an opportunity from another truck team to move on. It was really hard leaving Mike because I felt like he was one of the guys who really helped me get going and got me noticed.

How did the deal with Chip Ganassi Racing come about? I've heard that NASCAR vice president Jim Hunter recommended you for the ride.

That's kind of what they told me, that Jim had given me two thumbs up. I guess you could say he thought I was going to be a good driver and good for the sport. Chip and Felix [Sabates, co-owner] had been watching me and so had Tony [Glover] and Andy [Graves, team manager]. One thing Felix said to me that I really liked was, "You know, Jamie, you are

aggressive when you need to be and you get out of the way when you need to."

That's kind of the way I race. If I don't feel like I have a car that's capable of being where it is, I won't

Bobby Labonte, No. 18, provided McMurray's strongest challenge in the closing laps at Charlotte. *Sam Sharpe*

McMurray spent two mostly uneventful years in the Busch Series before landing a Winston Cup ride. *Sam Sharpe*

race somebody so hard and maybe have them get into me and get taken out. I'll let the guy go. That's kind of neat that they saw that and that they realized that. Obviously they wanted Ricky Rudd, and they were going to hire him and couldn't get everything worked out. You know, everything happens for a reason. I'm thrilled that it's happened. I don't know what I've done to deserve this opportunity, but I feel really blessed and I'm trying to make the most of it.

Considering the history of the Havoline car, which you'll be driving in 2003, do you feel added pressure to get the job done?

Most certainly. There have been so many great drivers in that car. To me, that's about the best sponsor in Cup, and for them to take a chance on a rookie, that meant a lot to me. But a sponsor can't put any more pressure on a driver than what a driver puts on himself. The thing is [that] there was a lot of pressure for me to perform in a Winston Cup car. Now that we've won a race it's almost a different type of pressure—just the pressure to keep performing and to live up to what I've already done. But really, and I've said this a million times to all the media, I'm just going to go out as a driver and give 100 percent, and the team is going to go out and give 100 percent. At the end of the day, if after every race, we can say that we did that, that's all we can do.

It was a great TV moment when they interviewed your dad after the win and you could see the emotion on his face. How instrumental has he been in your career?

Well, not just my dad but my whole family has been very supportive. My mom and dad gave up a lot to put me through the racing that I went through with go karts and stock cars. I would say my mom gave up a lot, maybe a new house or a new car, you know, just things you would like to have, just to get me to where I am. To have my dad there. . . . I had never won a truck race or a Busch race, so to get to have my dad there when I won my first race over the last couple of years, and to make it a Cup race of all things, that was really special. I didn't think about that until we got to victory lane and I saw my dad on the front row with a hat on, holding a No. 1 finger up and smiling for the camera. I don't know what was going through his head, but that was probably as important to me as anything, getting to see him there.

Did your dad race when you were younger?

My dad has raced since he was in high school. He did a lot of drag racing and stock car racing, just at the local level. When I became old enough to start racing, of course, I had a huge interest in it. My dad started racing go karts with me and we did that together for a long time. He actually gave it up for a while and just let me race. But it's in his blood and he still races go karts. He still goes and does that and has a great time at it. He just loves racing.

Talk about moving up to stock cars. Do you remember your first race?

We went to Lakeland, Florida, in 1994. My dad had bought a pavement Modified, and I remember it was so much different, (but) I just felt like I had a knack for it. The thing is, to me, to be good at any form of racing there has to be a huge level of dedication and desire. There's a lot of frustration that goes along with racing. You have to look past that. I've been very frustrated at times, but at the same time, throughout all of my racing, I was very dedicated and always tried to stay very focused at whatever I was doing. That's what I did when I moved up from go karts to stock cars. It was frustrating at first because it's so much different, and you go through a completely different learning curve. In go karts—at least when I raced go karts, although it's a lot different now—there weren't a lot of setups involved. You put tires on it and pretty much went out and raced it. Nowadays, they're so much different with setups and they scale them now and everything. When you move up to stock cars, there are springs and shocks and sway bars, so much stuff. So there was a lot to learn in that process.

How has your life changed since the fall of last year?

A lot more interviews. Of course, getting a ride with a team such as Ganassi and having Havoline as your sponsor, a lot of people question why they hired me. They're all wanting to know that. It's just been a lot busier. It's a good busy, like I say, but it didn't change a lot when I got hired. It was going to be pretty mellow, just running Talladega and a couple of other races. But, really, it changed after the win. It's been pretty wild, just the people who recognize you. In all my years of racing, I don't know that I've ever had anyone recognize me on an airplane, to just say "good job." Also the crewmembers and stuff who came up and said, "Man, we were on the edge of our seats." I've had so many people tell me they had goose bumps or it brought a tear to their eye. I can't tell you the way that makes me feel inside, to have a grown man tell me, "Man, I was crying for you, Jamie. I'm so happy for you." That's a feeling that I don't know I'll ever get again.

Is there any part of sudden fame that you would rather not have to deal with?

The thing is, like the interviews, maybe they are frustrating or aggravating because you have to do so many of them, but it's great to do interviews about positive stuff like this, versus doing interviews like a couple of months ago when they were asking me why Chip hired me. But I wouldn't change any of it. Every morning I wake up and I literally sit there and thank God for letting me feel as blessed as I feel right now. Like I say, I don't know what I did to deserve all this, because there are so many good race car drivers out there who never get the chance to keep moving up. And I don't know why I did. I don't know what I did different from those guys, because I don't feel like I did anything different. It's just an incredible situation that I got put into. Like I say, I don't know what I did to deserve it, but I'm certainly thankful for it.

The move from the Coors Dodge to the Havoline Dodge came complete with McMurray's upbeat personality.

Nigel Kinrade

RYAN NEWMAN

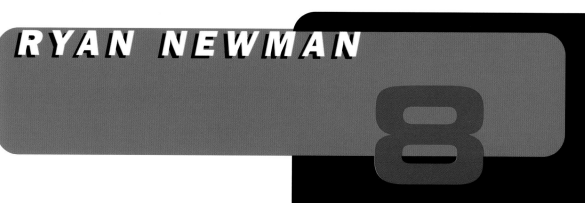

8

Born: December 8, 1977

Hometown: South Bend, Indiana

Height: 5-11

Weight: 207 lbs.

Sponsor	Alltel
Make	Dodge
Crew Chief	Matt Borland
Owner	Roger Penske

NASCAR Winston Cup Career Statistics

Year	Races	Wins	Top 5s	Top 10s	Poles	Total Points	Final Standing	Winnings
2000	1	0	0	0	0	40	70	$37,825
2001	7	0	2	2	1	497	49	$465,276
2002	36	1	14	22	6	4,593	6	$3,549,546
Totals	44	1	16	24	7	5,130		$4,052,647

Even though he cut his racing teeth in open-wheel cars, Ryan Newman always has been something of a natural-born stock car driver. *Harold Hinson*

ROGER AND RYAN

How Penske and Newman Cut a Contract

BY TERRY REED
From *Stock Car Racing*, December 2000

A graduate of the world-renowned engineering school at Indiana's Purdue University, Ryan Newman reminds many of the late Alan Kulwicki. *Harold Hinson*

under the tutelage of the Kenyon brothers and eventually won a dozen mains. From there, he excelled in sprint cars and managed himself well enough in championship dirt cars to become USAC's 1999 champion.

Looming large on his résumé is his pending degree in vehicle structure and engineering from Purdue University. It's an intimidating credential that to some folks implies that Newman carries in his head certain privileged and arcane secrets about the private lives of automobiles to which most people, even those absorbed in the technical nuances of the racing business, never will be apprised. The kid, one of his associates remarks, knows not only what a car is doing but also why it's doing it. Newman's left brain, in the meantime, has invited flattering comparisons with the famous left brain of Brown University mechanical engineer Mark Donohue, the fabled "Captain Nice" who joined Roger Penske in 1966 and won the Indianapolis 500.

At 22, South Bend, Indiana's Ryan Newman is one of auto racing's many purpose-bred circuit riders, the best known of whom is Jeff Gordon, who was "Shirley Templed" from birth, parentally programmed to be the pure and complete racing man, as unswervingly devoted to his calling as a monk to his breviary. Newman is perhaps as much the focused, conspicuously intelligent networker and politically correct self-spokesman that Gordon is, but he's also wryly whimsical, resolutely unflappable, understated, cagey, and dangerously astute.

That said, there is ironically little understood about Newman, who has been pounding the speedways for 17 gritty seasons after having been first lowered into a quarter-midget at age 4 1/2. At 17 he was the All-American Midget Series point man; at 19 he took on the USAC midget division

Going Cup

Newman never minced words about his Winston Cup ambitions, however. Before the 1997 season opened, he had engaged articulate fellow Hoosier Ben Dillon as his handler. This, by the way, is the same Dillon who, with Steve Horne, owned the financially distressed Tasman Motorsports outfit before it sold early last year to Forsythe Racing. While competing under the CART banner with Tasman, Dillon sat on CART's engine committee, where he became acquainted with Penske. Two years ago, Dillon commended Newman to Penske by way of mostly written documentation. Penske, in turn, referred the matter to his associate, Don Miller, part owner of Penske Racing South.

"Over time," Dillon says, "they became more interested in Ryan. When Ryan was running USAC open-wheel cars, they were pretty darned attentive. About nine months ago, we felt that Ryan was ready to move into NASCAR. We had more discussions with Roger, and Don Miller got more directly involved. He put together a very intelligent, correctly paced program for Ryan, involving testing for Penske South, and selected ARCA races this year. It was the perfect situation."

Newman recalls, "I first met Roger at the Daytona 500 this year. I met Don Miller the same day. Between Ben talking to Roger, Roger talking to Don, and Don looking out for future talent, all three of us had the same goal, which was for me to get some experience and laps so I could become a Winston Cup driver. I think they had scouts out."

Penske and company decided to send Newman out to mix it up with ARCA, whose cars are almost Winston-legal; that was six races into its 2000 season when it deployed at Michigan Speedway's two-mile high banks on June 10 for the Flagstar 200. By this time, Newman had tested a stock car for only three days there and at Gateway. Notwithstanding, he qualified second in the 41-car field, led laps 22 to 44, and came home seventh with a sour motor on the lead lap. "Newman's fault-free drive," Chris Economaki wrote, "came on a track twice as big as he'd ever driven before, against 40 drivers he'd never seen before, and at the wheel of a car weighing twice as much as he'd ever driven before."

At triangular Pocono on July 27, Newman started second again and made a mockery of the 80-lap Pepsi ARCA 200 after leading 40 circuits and goosing point leader, race leader, and 15-time ARCA winner Bob Strait straight out of the lead and hard into an inside wall with fewer than three laps remaining.

"It wasn't right to race like that," says the irate Strait, who lodged a futile complaint against Newman with ARCA.

"I hit a bump and got up into him, and you saw what happened," Newman says.

Fast Friends

When, on August 26, Newman tried his luck at the new 1 1/4 -mile Kentucky Speedway with crew chief Matt Borland, the former Pac West IndyCar man, they stole the pole and won the Blue Grass Quality Meats 200-miler. They also had at least two notables in tow. One was Penske himself who, for part of the race, acted as team spotter. The other was Elzie Wylie "Buddy" Baker, a massively built, easygoing, charismatic man who had come along as Newman's adviser.

Newman likens Baker, the 19-time NASCAR winner, to a "grandfather who looks over your shoulder. He's been there. He's done that. He knows what's going on." As for performing in front of the boss, he commented, "People think it's a lot of pressure," adding that it was an honor to have Mr. Penske on the premises.

After a last-lap threat from Tim Steele, the Michigan winner, Newman scored his second consecutive ARCA win, after which Penske jetted back to Bristol, where Winston Cupper Rusty Wallace brought him his second triumph of the day. For Newman, who held 38 other cars at bay for 83 of the race's 134 laps, it had been a perfect car and a perfect race.

Ryan Newman's Open-Wheel Roots

1993: All-American Midget Series Champion and Rookie of the Year

1995: USAC National Midget Series Rookie of the Year

1996: USAC Silver Crown Racing Rookie of the Year

1997: Established the all-time record for the fastest one-mile qualifying time for midgets (139.265 miles per hour)

1999: Sprint Car Rookie of the Year

"My crew chief and I and a couple of other guys on the team sat down last night and talked about our pit strategy," he explained afterward. "I listened to what they had to say. After that, it was basically common sense. This team is mostly young guys we put together to learn and grow together. My goal has always been stock car racing. We're doing this one step at a time."

In 1997, Newman established the all-time record for the fastest one-mile qualifying time for midgets with a time of 139.265 milers per hour. *Nigel Kinrade*

LIGHTNING STRIKES ONE MORE TIME

BY BOB MYERS
From *Circle Track*, April 2002

Indiana Native Ryan Newman Followed

His Head and His Heart in Chasing His NASCAR Dreams—

Now the Rest of the Field Just Might Be Chasing Him

Many people thought Newman would make his trip through Indianapolis Motor Speedway's Gasoline Alley in an Indy car. Newman knew better. *Harold Hinson*

Richard Petty has been retired as a driver for nine years and Dale Earnhardt is dead, but the legends continue to inspire young driving talent to race in NASCAR.

When Ryan Newman, a highly touted NASCAR and Winston Cup rookie at age 23, was a kid, the King and the Intimidator were his heroes. Newman attributes this admiration for planting a seed that he has nurtured to full bloom.

For Newman, born and raised in South Bend, Indiana, Indy cars were a natural progression. Starting before he was five, Newman raced open-wheel cars at several levels with increasing honors highlighted by the prestigious USAC Silver Crown championship in 1999.

"I think the dream to race Indy cars was there, but it wasn't as strong as racing in NASCAR at the Winston Cup level," Newman says. "I was sure of that about the middle of 1999."

Right Place, Right Time

As a timely and opportune result, Newman was signed in 2000 by owner Roger Penske to drive the No. 02 Penske Racing South/Alltel Fords in a limited schedule of ARCA, NASCAR Busch Series, and Winston Cup races leading to racing Winston Cup full time in 2002.

"Ryan is a very talented young driver, committed and focused," says Penske, who owns championship CART teams as well as principal interest in the Penske South Winston Cup team led by Rusty Wallace. "An acquaintance of mine sent me a résumé and recommended that I take a look at him. I watched him race a couple of times. He wanted to race in NASCAR, and

we thought it would be very positive to have a young driver coming up.

"He's doing really well. Based on what he's already shown, I think he can be a winner in Winston Cup, maybe next year. The younger guys seem to run their cars harder. Sometimes that's not good, but sometimes they wind up in the winner's circle quicker than expected. I think Ryan belongs in that group."

Don Miller, president and part-owner of Penske South, was actively involved in "recruiting" Newman and has taken not only a professional but almost fatherly interest in his and his youthful team's development.

"I watched Ryan race midgets and Silver Crown for two years and was very impressed before we arranged a test for him in a stock car, one of Rusty's old ones," Miller says. "He was outstanding in the test, so we went forward. After he finished seventh at Michigan in his first ARCA race and won his second at Pocono, signing him was a no-brainer.

"Along with immense talent and an uncanny ability to absorb everything you tell him and the next day put it to work, Ryan is a wonderful human being. He has high morals and values and one of the most infectious senses of humor I've ever seen in a person. He's an absolute pleasure to be around."

Obviously, Newman, who earned a degree in engineering from Purdue University in August, is thrilled.

"It's an honor and a blessing to be with Penske, Miller, and Wallace," Newman says. "And it's great to have Alltel as a sponsor because it gives us the opportunity to communicate with fans just like you talk on the telephone. I can't think of a better position to be in."

Richard Petty said often during his incomparable 35-year driving career that there is always somebody to replace you, no matter how good you are. "The talent is out there; we just don't always see it coming," the King says.

A Big Splash Indeed

Newman made such a big splash in stock cars that he appeared to competitors and fans to come out of nowhere. For example, October 2000 at Lowe's Motor Speedway, Newman earned the pole for a 100-mile ARCA race with a stock car track record of 186.780 miles per hour and led every lap. At Michigan in August 2001, he won his first Busch race, starting on the outside pole and leading 119 of 125 laps. In Winston Cup, he sat on the pole for the Coca-Cola 600 at Lowe's, though he crashed out of the race early while leading, and finished fifth in the June race at Michigan. All of this came after winning the season-opening ARCA 200 at Daytona International Speedway.

Statistically, Newman, in his first 20 starts for Penske South over two seasons, had four victories and four poles in seven ARCA races and a victory, three top 10s and three poles in nine Busch outings. In Winston Cup, he had one top five and a pole in four starts, including an inauspicious finish of 41st in his 2000 debut at Phoenix due to engine troubles.

Numbers are important but not of the essence for Newman and the Alltel team, led by crew chief Matt Borland, until this year. The objective in 2001 was experience—seat time for Newman in tests and races.

How's this for getting your season off to a great start? Newman won the season-opening ARCA race at Daytona International Speedway in 2001. *Sam Sharpe*

Newman has said that while his qualifying program is pretty well set he's still making mistakes in races. Here is one such occurrence.

Sam Sharpe

"I'm a rookie," Newman says. "Matt became a crew chief for the first time last year. We're a rookie team with an average age of about 27 and individual experience. But we have all the resources of a first-class, winning organization behind us.

"We've shown really strong points and some pretty serious weak points. I think winning the 600 pole at Charlotte and three poles in my first nine Busch races were great feats for the team. In the races, though, I've made a lot of mistakes that I don't ever want to make again. Spinning out all by myself on lap 11 of the 600 was a rookie mistake. There was no other excuse. I was impatient. If we can learn from our mistakes, we have had a great season."

Adjustment Period

Newman says his ability to drive, his reactions, and his feel for cars haven't changed, but adjusting to the characteristics of heavier stock cars and to the rigors of longer races has been difficult for him.

Newman and Borland, 30, an engineer with some open-wheel driving experience himself, didn't know each other until Newman came to Penske, but they have meshed. They communicate well in a language foreign to most except other engineers.

"Matt understands the physics of race cars and has a natural ability to understand math," Newman says. "Everyday life is all about math and numbers and how you can crunch them and do what you want. I'm really

happy he's my crew chief because of our background."

To be sure, Newman and the Alltel team are up to speed as qualifiers. "I think we have a great setup, be it the mechanics of the car," Newman says. "Qualifying is the only perfect situation you have for a race. You have all the downforce on the car, the tires are fresh, the air is clean, and you get to run as hard as you can by yourself for one or two laps."

Retired Winston Cup driver Buddy Baker, who excelled on the speedways before becoming a television analyst, is Newman's mentor. Baker is present for the initial tests at tracks new to Newman. He offers insight on how to approach and drive unfamiliar tracks and how cars react to tires and track surfaces. He preaches patience.

"Buddy has helped me a ton. If not for him, I'm sure I would have made more mistakes than I have in the car," Newman says. "He's a great coach and individual to have around."

Baker gives his student an A-plus. "He's going to be a superstar," Baker predicts. "I guarantee he will be as good as Jeff Gordon and Tony Stewart. But no matter what he accomplishes, he will be like Richard Petty in the respect that he'll never get the big head. If there is any such thing as a natural-born driver, he is. He's smart. He reminds me of [the late] Mark Donohue. He's fast and knows why. For a young driver, patience is a virtue. But I've also told Ryan that in order to make a good omelet, you have to break a few eggs. If he had spun out at Charlotte running 25th, nobody would have paid any attention."

Which prompts the question, how is the upper echelon treating Newman in his bid for respect and acceptance? "Treatment from other drivers has been up and down since I was involved in a scuffle in two early Busch races," Newman says. "But I think overall it's pretty good. I wouldn't expect everybody to like me, whether I'm a nice guy or not. And I don't know if I'm a nice guy."

Pleased with Progress

Borland is pleased with his driver's and team's progress. "Ryan is light-years ahead of where he was when we started in 2000, and he was pretty darn good then," Borland says. "He's gotten a good handle on how to drive these cars, and he is a lot more confident. He uses his head and doesn't lose his cool, which is something that's not common in a lot of drivers. He's definitely going to be one of the drivers to look at in the future. The guys are making changes a lot quicker, making fewer mistakes, improving pit stops. The team is jelling."

The fact that the team is a winner is no surprise to Newman. "I knew we had the potential," he says. "I can better evaluate after this year [2001], but I feel sure we can win in Winston Cup this year. We're preparing to run for the title. It will be difficult for essentially a rookie team, but I see no reason we can't do it."

John Erickson, general manager of Penske Racing South, adds perspective: "I don't think we could ask for better progression from the team overall, not just Ryan. Last year [2001] Ryan and the team have had more time to spend on cars and testing. This year [2002], the learning curve is going to be steeper considering the full Winston Cup schedule and some tracks that Ryan hasn't seen.

"I think Ryan has as much talent as some of the top rookies when they came in, but will we see it this year? That would be terrific, but we are not counting on it, and we're not going to tell the world. We don't want to put too much pressure on him. . . . Overall, we are confident Ryan will make a strong race for rookie of the year."

Family Affair

Newman raced his way to the big-league Penske organization in a small, close-knit family operation, consisting largely of his dad, Greg, who owns and operates an auto repair business; his mother, Diana, who worries about the dangers of racing; and his younger sister, Jamie, a college nursing student.

"My dad and grandparents were big racing fans who went to the Daytona 500 and Indy 500 every year," Newman says. "Dad wanted to drive but never had the opportunity. He said his firstborn was going to be a race car driver, so here I am. We spent a lot of weekends together at a lot of races as a family. I am very fortunate in that respect. My dad still comes to my races. He's the second gas-can man and does some pre-race spotting."

Newman and his parents mutually agreed that he should attend college. He didn't second-guess his

Being a driver for Penske Racing South has its advantages, as Newman talks racing with one of the best in the business—teammate Rusty Wallace (left)—daily. *Sam Sharpe*

Winning the pole for the Memorial Day Coca-Cola 600 at Lowe's Motor Speedway was a high point for Newman. Spinning out 11 laps into the 600-mile event three days later was the low point. *Sam Sharpe*

decision until he got to Purdue. Having to juggle school and racing, at one point he mulled dropping out but reconsidered. That was a prudent decision given the direct application of his vehicle structure engineering degree, which he completed via the Internet, to racing and the importance of image in the sport, he says.

Asked to describe himself, Newman, who is articulate, intelligent, personable, and built like a collegiate linebacker at 5-feet, 1-inches tall and 207 pounds, says, "I don't smoke or drink. I'm not a party person. I try not to do anything that distracts me from what I want to do. I enjoy fishing and spending time on the lake with friends and family. Matt and I have remote-control cars. I like music of the '50s and '60s, the Dave Matthews Band, comedy movies, and Pizza King pizza.

"I have a house on Lake Norman [near Mooresville, North Carolina, and the Penske shops] and clean it myself. That's good for me. It keeps me organized. It's kind of hard to know what you've got when somebody else is cleaning up your mess. . . . I guess I'm your normal different guy."

Different, perhaps, in the respect that Newman doesn't intend to marry. Don't misunderstand, he hastens to add. There are girls who are his friends with whom he hangs out, but his focus is on racing.

"By the time I'm 40, people will be living to 120. So I can get married when I am 60 and have kids when I'm 80," he says without cracking a smile. He admits the scenario is subject to change.

Newman has demonstrated an ability to listen and learn as a Winston Cup rookie. *Sam Sharpe*

All eyes will be on Newman as he heads into his second full season on the circuit. *Sam Sharpe*

ELLIOTT SADLER

9

Born: April 30, 1975

Hometown: Emporia, Virginia

Height: 6-2

Weight: 195 lbs.

Sponsor	M&Ms
Make	Ford
Crew Chief	Raymond Fox
Owner	Robert Yates

NASCAR Winston Cup Career Statistics

Year	Races	Wins	Top 5s	Top 10s	Poles	Total Points	Final Standing	Winnings
1998	2	0	0	0	0	128	59	$45,325
1999	34	0	0	1	0	3,191	24	$1,589,221
2000	33	0	0	1	0	2,762	29	$1,578,356
2001	36	1	2	2	0	3,471	20	$2,683,225
2002	36	0	2	7	0	3,418	23	$3,349,994
Totals	141	1	4	11	0	12,970		$9,246,121

Elliott Sadler's four-year stint in the No. 21 of Wood Brothers Racing marked his first full-time ride in Winston Cup. *John Pyle*

SADLER ON THE MOVE
TO YATES RACING

BY LARRY COTHREN
From *Stock Car Racing*, January 2003

All eyes will be on Elliott Sadler in 2003 as he moves from Wood Brothers Racing to debut the No. 38 M&M's Ford of Robert Yates Racing. Sadler took time recently to discuss his career move and proposed an interesting way for drivers to settle their differences. This interview was conducted by Larry Cothren.

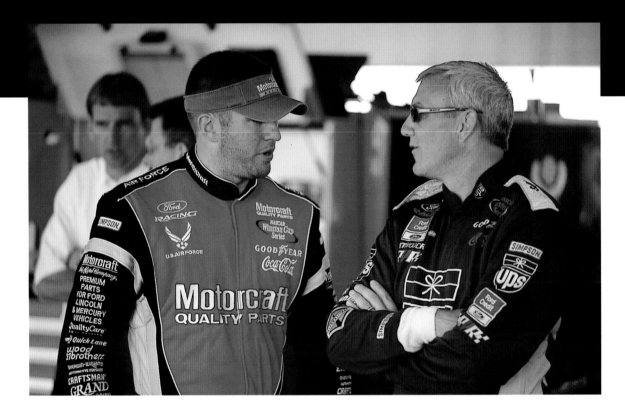

The opportunity to have Dale Jarrett (right) as a teammate factored heavily into Elliott Sadler's move to Robert Yates Racing. *Nigel Kinrade*

Was it difficult to go to Eddie and Len Wood early in 2002 and tell them you wanted out of your contract with Wood Brothers Racing?

That's by far the most difficult decision I've ever had to make, and by far the most difficult minute of my life when I took the time to tell Eddie at the airport in California, because they're just such great people. But I felt it was something I needed to do. I thought long and hard about it, but when the time came to make that decision—to actually go through with it—it was very tough internally.

How long did you agonize over that decision before you finally went through with it?

A few months, and then, finally, I wanted to save a sinking ship. We weren't running like we should have, and I was scared of Motorcraft pulling out and leaving the Wood brothers without a sponsor. I didn't want to be the person responsible for the Wood brothers losing their sponsor and maybe having to get out of racing. So I decided to step forward and ask for my release. Maybe it would give me some chances to go other places and also give them a chance to find a great driver for this race team.

It's almost like you single-handedly set Silly Season in motion. Were you surprised by the frenzy you triggered in the sport when you asked out of your contract?

I didn't know there were that many people paying attention to what was going on with my life and my career, but it got really hectic. Some of it was fun. I got to meet a lot of great people, a lot of great owners and sponsors. By meeting with some of the business managers, I really got to see the way a lot of different race teams are run and how they work. It was pretty neat, a good experience. There were some hard decisions to be made. When you've got friends involved with different race teams, it makes it tough sometimes, but it all worked out great.

How did you hook up with M&M's? How did that deal transpire?

Robert [Yates] called me and said he had a deal with a sponsor and wanted me to meet with these guys to do an interview deal and see if they liked me and if I fit in with what they were looking for. I can't remember exactly what race it was, but I had a meeting with Robert, Doug [Yates], and the M&M's people and just had a two-hour powwow on what could've, should've, or might happen in the future. I got a phone call a few days later saying they wanted to do the deal and we actually signed on the same day, M&M's and I did. So it was a pretty special day for all of us.

The rumor was that you were shopping around a sponsor. So apparently, it wasn't M&M's.

No, I didn't have any sponsors at all with me. That was one of the things that bothered me the most about Silly Season. Everybody was really hitting it on the head. The media was doing a good job on what was going on—other than that I had a sponsor with me. If I had a sponsor with me, I would have given it to my brother [Hermie] so he could run the full season. That would mean more to me than anything. But as far as my having anything with me, that never happened. That never came true or even was a possibility.

So Robert initiated the contact?

When he heard that I had asked for my release, of course, he knew and everybody else knew then that I was available. We started talking and thought that this might work or that might work, and I went to Dale Jarrett and asked him would he mind or would he give me his blessing if I came over there to be his team-mate. I asked him if he thought it would work and could we work together, and he said yeah. Robert and I kept talking and kept talking and it seemed like every-thing just fell right into place. I've made a lot of good friends over there so far, and I'm looking forward to racing with them.

What appealed to you most about Robert Yates Racing?

The biggest deal was how sincere he was when he was talking to me, Robert himself. When a car owner will sit there and tell you, "Hey, we're just going to try to outwork everybody else to stay ahead of the game," that really makes me feel good. And their engine program is second to none. That's something they take pride in, something they work hard at. Also, Fatback's [Michael McSwain's] attitude was a big part in it, how much he loves racing. Probably the biggest deal I really liked was Dale Jarrett as a teammate. He's a great guy, somebody I've always looked up to, and I think we're going to be great teammates together.

Given everything you experienced this year, do you ever look back and wish the sport were simpler, like back in the 1990s when you were running at South Boston Speedway in Virginia?

Yeah, this sport is definitely different. In the last five years it has grown so fast and times are changing so quick, it seems like every week there's something new that you need to be running on your car just to make it run fast. It's just a steady change in pace. It's very fast paced off the track as well as

The move to Robert Yates Racing gave Sadler a new look for 2003. *Harold Hinson*

on the track. Yes, it was a lot easier running South Boston in the 1990s, but you just have to keep up with the times.

What will you have to accomplish in 2003 before you consider it a success with Yates?

We need to finish in the top 10 in points, and I need to win some races. That's for my first year there. That's a championship contending team. Ricky [Rudd] has won a race in that car every year he's been over there and has led a ton of laps. Coming in there, I need to lead some races and run up front. I think we can do that. It's going to happen, but that's what we need to do to feel like we've done our job our first year together.

Given all that's gone on, with you and Ricky Rudd essentially trading rides, what's your relationship with Ricky like?

It's been fine. Business as usual. Ricky and I have always been friends and never had a cross word to say to each other about anything. I feel like I hit a home run with my deal, and I definitely feel like the Wood brothers hit a home run with Ricky. Eddie was the first person I called when I was going to sign my deal with Robert, and I think I was one of the first people he called when he got his deal done with Ricky. That's the kind of respect we have for each other. I think Ricky is going to help this program a lot with his experience. He's used to running his own team when he owned a single-car team, and I think the experience he's going to bring to this team is going to help these guys a lot.

Finish this statement: If I were Mike Helton, I would . . .

. . . knock down the bankings at Talladega and Daytona so everybody will quit crying about restrictor-plate racing.

So you think that's the best solution?

I don't know. I wouldn't want to be Mike Helton for all the money in the world. He's got the toughest job in racing. He's got 43 different owners and 43 different drivers pulling him in so many directions it's hard to make everybody happy, but he does a great job pacifying us. I tell you, he is definitely the right man for the job.

You made a perfect helmet toss at Ryan Newman's car during The Winston this year, blaming him for a crash that took you out of the race. Have you and Ryan mended fences since then?

Oh yeah. I was mad at him for what he did because we tore up a good race car, and it shouldn't have been torn up. I was really upset about that because the guys work so hard in the shop to put these things together. We've talked since then and everything is fine and we haven't had a minute's trouble since then. It was just a heat-of-the-moment deal. I probably should not have done it but it was The Winston, with a lot of money on the line, and it's for the fans, so I thought the fans might get a kick out of it.

Would you like to see the helmet toss become part of the pre-race show?

Yeah, I think I can throw a helmet a right good ways, or throw it pretty hard, so I might have a chance to win something like that.

You were pretty accurate, too.

I played baseball all through my whole life and I play softball now. I thought if I didn't throw it like I was supposed to, they might kick me off the softball team.

Are you NASCAR's biggest wrestling fan?

Oh yeah. I probably know a lot more about wrestling than some of the other guys in the garage.

I do a lot of stuff backstage with them and know the guys on a personal level. I think that gives me the inside track on what's going on in wrestling.

Any similarities between NASCAR and the WWE?

I think sometimes after some of these short-track races we ought to set up a wrestling ring and let everybody go at it instead of throwing helmets and booties and hand gestures and stuff like that. Just let the fans stay there, set up a ring in the middle of the track, and let us go at it.

Would you rather wrestle Ward Burton or Jimmy Spencer?

I would like to try Jimmy Spencer. I like Ward. He's from Virginia. I probably could toss him around a little easier, but I would like to try Jimmy. He's a big boy, and I would like to get him in there and see what he's got.

You mentioned baseball. Did you play any other sports in high school?

I played baseball, basketball, football, cross-country, golf, and soccer. I played all those in high school.

Did you follow racing closely while growing up?

Yes. I had three uncles who raced. My dad raced. My brother raced. I've got five first cousins who race now. We always followed racing. I used to go to Richmond and buy tickets just like everybody else. I used to go to

"I didn't want to be the person responsible for the Wood brothers losing their sponsor and maybe having to get out of racing."

—Elliott Sadler

Rockingham, used to go to Martinsville, used to go to North Wilkesboro. There were a lot of different places we used to go to watch the races. I was a big fan long before I was able to participate in this sport.

Who was your favorite driver?

I liked Cale Yarborough growing up, and I liked Sam Ard a ton in the Sportsman Division, what is now the Busch Series. I was a huge, huge Sam Ard fan.

What current or former driver do you try to mold yourself after?

I have all the respect in the world for everybody who drives in NASCAR, but the guy I really like emulating the most is D. J. [Dale Jarrett]. What he does off the track and the type of personality he has and what he stands for and the way he's represented this sport is second to none. If there's anybody I would try to mold myself after, it would be him.

And the whole world awaits the answer to this one: What's your favorite color M&M?

I like the green one right now. The green one, she's looking pretty good. Back when I was growing up, if you had a green M&M you were supposed to hit a home run, so green has always been my favorite.

I hear there's a new M&M's paint scheme on tap for next year.

They've got some pretty cool paint schemes lined up for next year. I think everybody is going to enjoy them. They've done some cool stuff with the charac-

ters on the car, and I think everybody is going to get a pretty good kick out of it.

Look for a green No. 38, I take it?

It looks good.

Sadler and Yates have the opportunity to establish a new identity with the No. 38 M&M's Ford. *Sam Sharpe*

Sadler and Dale Earnhardt Jr. (left) swap secrets. *Nigel Kinrade*

SCOTT WIMMER

10

Born: January 26, 1976

Hometown: Wausau, Wisconsin

Height: 6-0

Weight: 175 lbs.

Sponsor	Stacker2/StaminaRX
Make	Chevrolet
Crew Chief	Chris Rice
Owner	Gail Davis

NASCAR Winston Cup Career Statistics

Year	Races	Wins	Top 5s	Top 10s	Poles	Total Points	Final Standing	Winnings
2000	1	0	0	0	0	0*	74	$37,780
2002	3	0	0	0	0	192	56	$143,110
Totals	4	0	0	0	0	192		$180,890

* —Ran the NAPA 500 at Atlanta but was not awarded points due to late entry (NASCAR mandates drivers declare entry 13 days prior to event).

"All I want to do is race," says Scott Wimmer. *Greg Aleck*

WORKING FOR A LIVING

BY GREG ALECK
From *Stock Car Racing*, December 2000

ASA Driver Scott Wimmer Is Building a Career One Series at a Time

Scott Wimmer has become accustomed to post-race celebrations. *Mike Slade*

T he middle child of three sons and one daughter born to Joan and Ron Wimmer, Scott Wimmer was born on January 26, 1976, in Wausau, Wisconsin, where he resides today.

He is the nephew of legendary Midwest racer Larry Detjens and Scott's interest in racing stemmed from birth. Wimmer followed in his uncle's footsteps and at age four began competing as a downhill skier, just as Detjens had in his youth. He would continue to compete in the sport for years, and in 1990 won the Central United States Ski Association divisionals and finished 13th (out of 150 skiers) in the 1990 Junior Olympics in Winter Park, Colorado.

But it was in 1981, when Scott was six years old, that Detjens was killed in a racing accident at Wisconsin International Raceway (WIR). While challenging for the lead, Detjens and Alan Kulwicki made contact, both spinning into the backstretch guardrail, killing Detjens instantly. To honor his uncle's memory, Wimmer returns annually to run in the Larry Detjens Memorial race at WIR. "I was there that day," says Wimmer. "It's still scary for me every time I go out there."

The Early Years

At the age of eight, Wimmer began racing three-wheel ATVs alongside five-year-old brother Chris. Between 1983 and 1984, Scott won three national championship classes in the amateur three-wheel ATVs.

Then in 1990 at age 14, Wimmer began his auto racing career, when his dad, Ron, bought him a stock car to compete in the local Sportsman division.

"We only ran a couple of races that year because Scott was also playing football in high school, and near the end of the season he was involved in an accident at Wausau's State Park Speedway," Ron recalls.

"I was racing at Wausau in 1990 in the Sportsman division," adds Scott. "I spun out; this guy came into the corner and hit me in the driver-side door. A piece of his frame came through and hit me in the leg. It cut me up pretty bad, and I didn't race anymore that season."

"After the accident, he needed to decide for himself if he still wanted to race," his father explains. "It was a freak thing that happened. It blew his calf muscle right out, and after they stitched him up, he was scared and in a lot of pain. It took some time for him to make up his mind. But finally, he came to me and said, 'Yeah, I want to go back to racing.' "

In 1992 Ron and the team rebuilt his wrecked racer, and Scott began to win many local Sportsman races. They bought a new Sportsman car in 1993, and Scott added more wins. His career was in motion.

Wimmer switched to the late-model and super late-model ranks in 1994 and took multiple rookie-of-the-year honors and numerous features each year.

In 1997 he began racing with the Hooters Cup series, where his performance earned him sponsorship from Jackaroo Gold Sauces (the distributor for Hooters' retail products) to run a new Monte Carlo in the Hooters ProCup series in its inaugural year (1998).

He prepared a new Monte Carlo for the 1999 season, but without the Jackaroo sponsorship, and struggled on the lower budget. At the end of the season, Ron felt that Scott and the team needed to leave the series.

"The engine budget for 1999 was more than $100,000 dollars, and we had to make a change," says Ron. "The sponsorship dollars couldn't keep pace with the expenses we had to be competitive. That's when we heard about the new ASA spec engine/tire format for 2000, and Scott had wanted to compete in ASA. We've always said if we're going to race, we should always do it with the best."

For 2000 the shy, soft-spoken 24-year-old moved to the ASA ACDelco Series. He became only the second driver in series history to win two consecutive races in his rookie year.

At this writing, Wimmer leads the Pat Schauer Memorial Rookie of the Year Championship by 88 points over a tough class of rookies, including Larry Foyt (A. J.'s son), David Bonnet (Neil's son), Mark E. Dismore (as in IRL), Paul Dallenbach (Wally's youngest son), and his closest rival, Robbie Pyle, driving the Young Motorsports Chevrolet. He sits in sixth place, 335 points from leader Gary St. Amant.

The 2000 Season

Wimmer has had a good year, and he's quick to thank his crew, at the same time demonstrating his family's involvement in his career.

"There's my mom, Joan [spotter]; dad, Ron [crew chief]; brother, Chris; Dave Pagel, Jason Redding, Flip Merwin, and Bill Stevenson [tire changers]; Mike Beyer, Scott Fouscro [jack men]; Todd Holerud, Carrol Bird [gas men]; Joe Betla, Dave Allen [tire carrier]," he continues, "and the ladies: Jody Ambrose, Ann

Stevenson [scorers]; Samantha Wimmer, Linda Bird [catch can], and finally my aunt, Margo Detjens [stop sign/catch can].

"Originally, our goal was to go to Lakeland [season opening BF Goodrich 300] and see how we'd run; I've raced and won there before. We were going to run just six to eight races to keep my rookie status for 2001," Scott says. "We thought we'd be competitive—you know, a top five or 10 finish.

"I didn't qualify that well, so we had to run the qualifying race. I was leading the race, and a bolt comes off another car, goes through the radiator, the motor starts to overheat and shuts down, and we missed the race.

The 2002 Busch season brought a breakthrough performance for Wimmer. *Harold Hinson*

Team owners Gail and Bill Davis hail from the ASA ranks, like Wimmer. *Harold Hinson*

"Since we missed the show at Lakeland, we decided to go to Lanier for the Discount Auto Parts 300 and won the race. That was one of the greatest thrills of my life—my late Uncle Larry was smiling down on me that day. For me to race against ASA's best and beat them fair and square was great!" The best are both former ASA ACDelco champions Mike Miller (in second) and Butch Miller (in third).

"He had us beat," says Mike. "I'm tickled to death for Scott. I raced against his uncle many times, and I'll tell you he's proud of this nephew today."

"After the win at Lanier, we had to go to Hickory. I'd also raced there in my ProCup days and knew the track fairly well," Scott says.

With one win under their belt, Wimmer and the team set off to Hickory, North Carolina, for the Jani-King 300, where they qualified in 11th position.

With four wins in the final eight Busch races in 2002, Wimmer had plenty to celebrate.

Harold Hinson

Conserving his car for the better part of the race, Wimmer took the lead with 66 circuits remaining to claim his second consecutive ASA victory.

As racing goes, the next eight races weren't as earthshaking as his first two, with finishing spots ranging from 2nd to 30th.

The Future

"All I want to do is race—my father has given me the chance to compete in some of the best oval-track series in the country, learning from the best," Wimmer says with a smile. "My family, friends, and our local sponsors have helped me so much over the years that I could never do enough to repay them. I've really been blessed."

The young driver adds, "After the Hickory win, I got calls from several NASCAR teams: Bill Davis Racing and Roush Racing. I've tested a truck for Jack Roush, and the test went great. After I talked to Bill Davis, he sent his plane and flew us to South Boston Speedway, and I tested in the ATT Busch car that they field. I felt real comfortable in the car, and they really liked how I did.

"Bill and his whole team are great. They're trying to help us find a sponsor for the ASA car and want me to finish out the year and try to win the rookie-of-the-year title. He's offered me a five-race deal this year with an option for next year, and my first race is at Richmond, September 9."

"Bill Davis came from our stomping grounds," adds Ron. "He was in ASA back when Mark Martin ran here, and he knew Scott was Larry's [Detjens] nephew. Also, Dick Trickle and other current Busch Grand National drivers have raced against him, so he knew he had the talent. I think the deal we have with Bill Davis is the best we could dream for. He has a great bunch of guys on the team and great equipment. They're just our kind of people, like family."

Wimmer's Career Stats

1994: Six late-model wins (20 top fives); State Park Speedway Rookie of the Year; State Park Speedway Driver of Tomorrow; second-place points finish (Dells Motor Speedway); Late Models Dells Motor Speedway Rookie of the Year; Wisconsin Short Track Series Rookie of the Year

1995: Two late-model wins (23 top fives); Country Time Series Overall Champion; second-place points finish in Dells Motor Speedway late models; tenth overall in the Miller Nationals at Slinger/Madison Speedway

1996: Nine late-model wins (47 top fives); Dells Motor Speedway late-model points champion; Miller Triple Crown champion (Dells Speedway); second-place finish in the Budweiser Triple Crown (Dells Speedway); tied for win of the Coca-Cola Triple Crown Series (Slinger Speedway); 2nd-place finish in the World Series of Asphalt (New Smyrna Speedway)

1997: Three late-model wins (18 top fives); Hooters ProCup Late Model Series Rookie of the Year; seventh place in the Hooters Cup points championship; third overall in the Miller Nationals (Slinger Speedway); Round 2 winner of the Miller Lite Triple Crown

1998: Two Hooters ProCup wins; four late-model wins (nine top fives); fifth place in the Hooters ProCup points championship; Hooters ProCup Hard Charger of the Year

1999: Won three races, including two Hooters Pro Cup Series races, at Langley Speedway and Lakeland Speedway; finished 11th overall in Hooter's Pro Cup final point standings

2000: Competed full time in the American Speed Association (ASA); won the first two races that he entered that season, at Lanier Speedway and Hickory Motor Speedway

2001: Competed in his first full season of NASCAR Busch Series competition; logged two top-5 and eight top-10 finishes. Finished 11th in the final point standings

2002: Competed in his sophomore season of NASCAR Busch Series competition; scored four wins: Dover, Memphis, Phoenix, and Homestead; finished career high third in the final point standings

INDEX